POET & ARTIST
Imaging the *Aeneid*

Text and CD-Rom prepared by

Henry V. Bender, Ph.D. & David J. Califf, Ph.D.

Bolchazy-Carducci Publishers, Inc.
Wauconda, Illinois USA

Editor:
LeaAnn A. Osburn

Cover Design & Typography:
Adam Philip Velez

Cover Illustration:
The Opening Engraving in the 1698 Dryden edition

Poet & Artist
Imaging the Aeneid
Henry V. Bender, Ph.D. & David J. Califf, Ph.D.

Bolchazy-Carducci Publishers, Inc.
1000 Brown Street, Unit 101
Wauconda, Illinois 60084
www.bolchazy.com

Printed in the United States of America
2004
by Publishers Graphics

ISBN 0-86516-585-8

Library of Congress Cataloging-in-Publication Data
Virgil.
 [Aeneis. Selections]
 Poet & artist : imaging the Aeneid / text and CD-Rom prepared by Henry V. Bender & David J. Califf.
  p. cm.
 Selections from Books 1, 2, 4, 6, 10, and 12.
 Latin text; commentary and discussion questions in English.
 CD-Rom contains illustrations drawn from the 1698, 2nd ed. of John Dryden's translation of the works of Virgil.
 ISBN 0-86516-585-8 (pbk. with CD)
 1. Aeneas (Legendary character)--Poetry. 2. Virgil. Aeneis--Examinations, questions, etc. 3. Aeneas (Legendary character)--Art. 4. Virgil. Aeneis--Illustrations. 5. Latin language--Readers. 6. Epic poetry, Latin. I. Title: Poet and artist. II. Bender, Henry V., 1945- III. Califf, David J. IV. Title.

PA6801.A7 2004
872'.01--dc22

                                        2004011500

POET & ARTIST

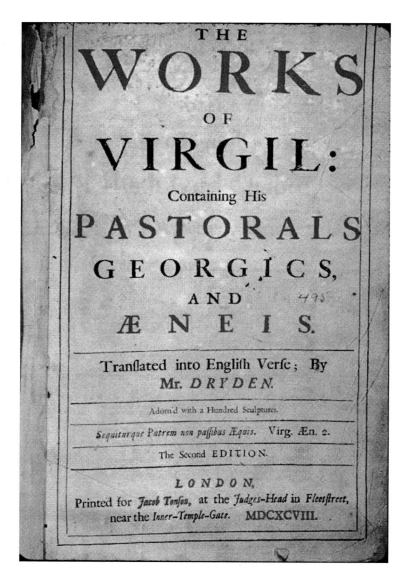

THE
WORKS
OF
VIRGIL:
Containing His
PASTORALS
GEORGICS,
AND
ÆNEIS.

Translated into English Verse; By
Mr. DRYDEN.

Adorn'd with a Hundred Sculptures.

Sequiturque Patrem non passibus Æquis. Virg. Æn. 2.

The Second EDITION.

LONDON,
Printed for Jacob Tonson, at the Judges-Head in Fleetstreet,
near the Inner-Temple-Gate. MDCXCVIII.

Title page from John Dryden's *The Works of Vergil: Containing His Pastorals and Georgics and Aeneis,* 2nd ed. (London:by Jacob Tonson, 1698).

~ CONTENTS ~

Preface   vii

Introduction   xi

Book I, *Aeneid,* Latin text and discussion questions   1

Book II, *Aeneid,* Latin text and discussion questions   21

Book IV, *Aeneid,* Latin text and discussion questions   33

Book VI, *Aeneid,* Latin text and discussion questions   49

Book X, *Aeneid,* Latin text and discussion questions   63

Book XII, *Aeneid,* Latin text and discussion questions   67

Appendix:
An Annotated List of the Illustrations from Dryden's translation of the *Aeneid.*   73

Instructions for Using the CD of Illustrations (included in this book)   88

❦ PREFACE ❦

In 1698 John Dryden published a second edition of his translation of the works of Publius Vergilius Maro. Both editions contained excellent full page illustrations coordinated with specific points in the Latin text. There are 71 such illustrations for the *Aeneid*. They serve as effective visual enactments of Vergil's narrative, but they also function as mirrors of the cultural values and the artistic development of the late 17th century in Western Europe.

Believing that these illustrations could be of great service to students and teachers of the *Aeneid* at any level, I set out on a project which has culminated in the present work (text and CD), an undertaking that consumed the past five years. There were several stages. Using excellent equipment, I made 35 mm slides of each illustration in Dryden's *Aeneid*. Each illustration appears at first in its entirety, bearing the dedication that was inserted into the space at the bottom of the folia. Then, each appears without the dedication, and, finally, subsequent exposures reveal various close-ups of particularly significant details or figures. Consequently, each single full-size folium includes as many as five slides, depending upon the intricacy and the significance of each illustration. A list of the folia with their dedications exactly as they appear in Dryden accompanies this text.

The second stage of the project consisted of digitizing each exposure. In this endeavor I am grateful to Mr. Richard Bauer, Chief Information Officer at The Hill School, and Mr. David Allain, Supervisor of the Digital Arts Annex at The Hill School. The generosity of these two individuals and their patience with me over a two-year period was truly commendable. Together we created for the first time a superb collection of digitized slide images to accompany the study and teaching of the *Aeneid*.

As the imaging portion of this project came to a close, other questions arose such as who did the illustrations or who made the engravings. I am grateful to have had the pleasure of working with Dr. David Califf, whose background and special interests include printmaking, book-making, and Roman epic. This happy coincidence of special interests allowed us to answer these questions through research. We discovered, as his subsequent article in this book demonstrates, that the illustrations in Dryden's *Aeneid* were not done or created for that text. In fact, these illustrations first appear in 1654 in John Ogilby's prose translation of the *Aeneid*.

Further research demonstrated that Dryden's publisher in 1697 and again in 1698, took these drawings and etched into their plates specific line references where the illustrations made the strongest connection with the Vergilian narrative. Some illustrations respond to a small number of lines and basically present one scene. Others, frankly the majority, are telescopic, as they are informed by a series of events in a specific place. For example, the illustration showing Aeneas escaping from Troy emphasizes the moment of departure. Set against the background of the burning city, Creusa follows Aeneas, who carries Anchises, and who escorts Ascanius. The illustrator omits some of the narrative details that Vergil supplies.

Precisely this kind of editorial, artistic choice can be most illuminating to both a student and a teacher. The teacher, familiar with the entire Vergilian story, and cognizant of the reception of Vergil by subsequent ages, easily sees the correlation of many sources for each illustration. In the escape from Troy, the engraver renders the figure of Creusa with her right hand placed over her chest, her head bent down towards the surface of the ground, and with an angelic, almost divine, countenance, suggestive of the female images attributed to Renaissance painters such as Botticelli or even Da Vinci. These stunning characteristics offer an interpretative avenue for the teacher and the class to explore. What is the engraver trying to portray? By his carvings, the engraver alludes to Creusa's impending death and creates a visual foreshadowing which reflects the artist's knowledge of her fate.

Once the 71 images that adorn the 1698 Dryden's *Aeneid* formed a digitized whole, I created a PowerPoint presentation of those images, arranged and divided according to each book of the *Aeneid* in the sequence of their order in the original edition of Dryden. Since most teachers of the *Aeneid* in secondary schools will be concerned about completing the lines of the Advanced Placement* (AP) syllabus, I made additional PowerPoint presentations titled and corresponding strictly to the books and lines that constitute the current AP syllabus. Therefore, the accompanying CD features PowerPoint presentations for Books 1 through 12 with every image and its close-ups. The PowerPoint presentations for the AP contain only those images that correspond to the current AP Vergil syllabus.

To make this CD most useful and instructive, I included, in a workbook style format, all of the Latin lines that constitute the current AP syllabus. The rationale for this was simple. Wherever one of the illustrations seemed to belong, the title of the illustration was to be inserted in that text, and the corresponding Latin lines would then be italicized. With the Latin text at a student's fingertips, viewing the projected image from a CD would be a far more instructive and efficient classroom experience. Students could immediately look at the images and connect them with the text. This innovation invariably led us to a further step.

When Dr. Ladislaus Bolchazy examined this project, he suggested that discussion questions be written to prompt and facilitate both teacher and student comprehension of the connections between the images and the text they portray. The response became the extensive series of analytical questions that accompany each illustration. These questions invite students to explore the images that they are facing. We have designed these questions to promote deeper understanding of the meaning of the Latin that each student has translated. In many cases, the associations between text and image, between poet and artist, are made clear after a reflective study.

Students need space to write down their responses, particularly in a classroom setting. As a veteran teacher, I am very sensitive to the problems that can develop when you ask a student to take out one book, and then another book, and then a notebook, and expect the student not only to pay close attention to something that is projected on the screen, but also to find an extraordinary amount of open space on their desk. Therefore, we have developed the text to function as a classroom workbook.

Discussion questions appear on the left pages of the book, and the Latin text appears on the right pages. Students use the open white space on the left pages to write down reactions, to answer questions, and to complete homework assignments. This format allows the text to be used efficiently both in class and at home. In class, teachers enjoy the advantage of quick reference to the Latin text to exercise their students on the translation of the Latin into English without the presence of any vocabulary or grammatical prompts. In moments of review, the textbook also provides the advantage of allowing the student to write down either immediate or researched responses to the posed questions. Teachers can even collect these texts and can mark the pages on which the students have supplied their answers.

*AP is a registered trademark of the College Entrance Examination Board, which was not involved in the production of, and does not endorse, this product.

How to Use This Book

For the teacher:

The teacher's goal in this exercise should be to probe the depth of a student's familiarity and command of the original Latin of Vergil. The teacher projects an image of choice from the CD and then tells students to turn their manuals to the section of text that is represented by the image. At this point, the teacher asks the class to select from their Latin text specific words that can be found illustrated in the projected drawing. The teacher should prompt the students to *actually* make connections between word and image. In this process, some key Latin words will not be illustrated. This offers the opportunity for a teacher to discuss why the artist may have treated those words so quietly. For homework, the teacher may assign other images on the CD, relevant to the passage of the text, to be studied by the student. In the next class meeting, a fruitful discussion on that or another related slide can take place. The teacher may instruct students to write their responses for homework on the white space below questions that appear on the left-hand pages of the text, or compose essay responses to those questions.

For the student:

Students should familiarize themselves with the images on the CD *after* they have studied the Latin text. Working to render a good English translation of the Latin lines, students confront the precise ways in which the Latin finds expression in the drawing. The goal of a student should always be to look at this interaction, to probe the way in which the written word of Vergil has informed the drawing. By looking at the images students should be able to retain a grasp of the sequence and development of the plot of the *Aeneid*. The visual images themselves simultaneously generate both a sense of the whole as well as a command of the specific. Students should also frequently turn to this manual to review the Latin itself without access to any commentary or vocabulary. This process is an excellent way of solidifying knowledge of Latin, as it encourages the effort of translation, understanding, and comprehension without any assistance—the ultimate benchmark of the student's capabilities in Latin. In the use of both the CD and the text, many additional questions may occur to students. These questions may be written down and brought to the attention of fellow students and the classroom teacher in the spirit of intellectual inquiry that should characterize the study of this great work of literature.

I sincerely hope that this text and CD will both facilitate the continued teaching of the *Aeneid* as well as foster a new level of understanding, promoting the ultimate integration of the arts and the word or in short, the roles of the poet and the artist in the imaging of the *Aeneid*.

Henry V. Bender, Ph.D.
Elizabeth Blossom Chair of Humanities
Isaac Thomas Chair of Classics
The Hill School

Adjunct Professor of Classics
St. Joseph's University and Villanova University

Introduction

Illustrating the *Aeneid*

John Dryden's *Works of Virgil* is perhaps the most widely known and admired English translation of a classical Latin author. A seminal work in the history of Vergil reception, Dryden's translation is also fine English poetry in its own right. Despite the high regard in which Dryden's *Virgil* is justly held, the illustrations that accompanied his translation are all but unknown to modern classicists. The text and CD, *Poet and Artist: Imaging the Aeneid*, strive to bring these magnificent images out of obscurity so that they may be seen, studied, and used by teachers, students, and scholars alike. This brief introductory essay provides the background information necessary for a better appreciation of Dryden's illustrated text.

The Translations

Vergil's *Aeneid* is one of those rare literary works that attained "classic" status before it was even finished. Indeed, Vergil became a canonical author taught in the schools by 25 B.C.E., still within the poet's lifetime, and Propertius wrote of the epic in progress as "something greater than the *Iliad*" (*nescioquid maius … Iliade*, 2.34.66). Vergil imitators abounded in ancient Rome, and Latin hexameters written today continue to be judged by the Vergilian standard. After the *Aeneid*, any serious epic poet — from Ovid, Lucan, and Statius to Dante, Milton, and Tasso, to Pound — has had to grapple with Vergil's imposing legacy. Moreover, the poet's significance for the western literary tradition as a whole is so profound and pervasive that it arguably extends even to writers with little or no first-hand knowledge of Rome's great master.

While Vergil's afterlife is too wide-ranging, too diverse and complex to be mapped out in a coherent fashion, the history of *Aeneid* translations is comparatively easy to trace. We know that in antiquity the *Georgics* were translated into Greek, the *lingua franca* of the Mediterranean. It is possible that the *Aeneid*, or parts of it, enjoyed the same fate. On the other hand, the increasing dominance of Latin and the early acceptance of Vergil as a preeminent writer in that language may account for the general lack of extant *Aeneid* translations before the modern era.

The first complete translation of the *Aeneid* to be published in Britain was written in Scottish verse by Gavin Douglas. Completed in 1513, it remained unpublished for forty years and appeared for the first time in 1553.

The first complete English verse translation of the *Aeneid* was published in 1573. Nearly twenty years earlier, Thomas Phaer had undertaken the project, perhaps encouraged by the arrival of the Douglas translation. Phaer published his rendition of books one through seven in 1558. In 1562, he added books eight and nine and part of book ten. Thomas Twyne finished the translation in 1573, adding Maffeo Vegio's thirteenth book in 1584 and revising Phaer's work along the way.

In the first half of the 17ᵗʰ century, poets such as Jonson, Sandys, and Cowley translated excerpts from the *Aeneid*, but it was John Ogilby who composed the next English verse translation of the full epic, to which he added the *Eclogues* and *Georgics*. Ogilby's *Virgil* was first published by Thomas Crook in 1649 and was subsequently issued by

Andrew Crook in 1650 and 1665. In 1654, however, Ogilby produced a second and substantially different complete Vergil translation, this one accompanied by a set of one hundred magnificent illustrations or "sculptures" (i.e. engravings) as they were called in the seventeenth century. The illustrated Ogilby translation was first published by Thomas Warren and later by Thomas Roycroft (1658, 1663, 1668), Parker and Guy (1675), and Thomas Guy alone (1684).

John Dryden was famously critical of Ogilby's translation, and he did not like the current French and Italian versions much better. Thus, he set to work on his own translation, which was published by Jacob Tonson in 1697 and reissued in 1698.

By the time he decided to translate Vergil, Dryden was already a celebrated poet. Born in 1631, Dryden was one of the leading literary figures of the Restoration era. He spent his early career writing for the theater, and his success in that sphere led to his appointments as poet laureate (1668) and historiographer royal (1670) under Charles II. Dryden rose to prominence as a literary critic with his essay "Of Dramatick Poesie," but during the turbulent decade of the 1680s, his writings took on a more overtly political character. Under William III, the poet fell out of political favor and spent the last part of his career as a translator of ancient texts. By far, his most extensive and important translation project was *The Works of Virgil*, but Dryden made English versions of other authors as well. His success as a satirist no doubt contributed to the quality of his Persius and Juvenal translations, and his *Fables* of Homer, Ovid, Boccaccio, and Chaucer are equally noteworthy. Today, Dryden is perhaps best remembered for "Absalom and Achitophel," "Alexander's Feast," and "Of Dramatick Poesie," as well as his *Virgil*.

The Prints

The idea of illustrating the *Aeneid* was by no means novel in the 17th century. Illustrated Vergil texts date back at least to the 4th or 5th century CE, and we are fortunate that two manuscripts from that era have survived. (Images from one of them, the so-called "Vatican Vergil," are currently available on the Vatican's website.) Medieval and Renaissance illustrations are also extant, but it was the rise of printmaking in the 16th century that made illustrated books of all types a relatively common commodity.

Many hands were involved in producing the illustrations that accompany the Ogilby and Dryden Vergil translations. We know the names of four: Francis Cleyn, Wenceslaus Hollar, Pierre Lombart, and William Faithorne. Each was a respected artist in his day, and each contributed something distinctive to the project. In addition, at least one unknown hand was responsible for reworking the plates and providing the new inscriptions that would accompany the illustrations in Dryden's version.

Francis Cleyn was born in Rostock, Germany, in a year variously given as 1582, 1590, and an implausible 1600. Skilled as a painter, illustrator, and graphic artist, Cleyn made his principal living as an interior designer. After a period of study in Rome, he moved to England, where he worked for Kings James I and Charles I. His duties included the design of tapestries and architectural ornaments as well as the interior decoration of palaces. A lover of the classics, Cleyn also found time to illustrate Homer's *Iliad*, Aesop's *Fables*, Ovid's *Metamorphoses*, and, of course, Vergil's *Aeneid* before his death in 1658.

All of the Vergil plates, which include attribution, name Cleyn as the *inventor*, or "designer." (The Latin verb *invenire*, "to find" or "discover," was typically used in the printmaking business to mean "design.") Thus, Cleyn is the artist who conceived and drafted the original images. He produced a series of drawings, which the other artists copied and executed as prints. Regrettably, few of Cleyn's original Vergil drawings survive, but two are housed in Oxford's Ashmolean Museum: "The Punishment of Laocoon" and "The Funeral of Misenus." Both drawings are crowded with illustrative detail, as was typical in the 17th century, yet Cleyn's pen is remarkably delicate, his tone values subtle yet lucid. Because these drawings were copied directly onto the engraving plates, they appear as mirror images of the final prints.

Wenceslaus Hollar was born in Prague in 1607. He studied drawing and engraving in Frankfurt with Matthäus Merian, an artist well-respected in the 17th century but largely forgotten today. In 1625, Hollar published his first plates, "The Virgin and Child" and "Ecce Homo." For the next decade or so, the young artist traveled throughout northern Europe and quickly established a reputation as a distinguished draftsman and engraver of urban scenes. He also sketched the great paintings he encountered in his travels, and it is this skill that brought him to the attention of the Earl of Arundel, who became his patron. In 1637, Hollar accompanied the earl to England, where he became a royal draftsman in the court of Charles II and eventually earned the title of "His Majesty's Scenographer and Designer of Prospects." Although he was a prolific artist who produced nearly 3000 different images, Wenceslaus Hollar died in poverty in 1677. Today he is best remembered for his English portraits and views of London. Stylistically, Hollar's work is characterized by a graceful and fluid line, meticulous attention to detail, and great technical security in execution.

Pierre Lombart was born in Paris. The year of his birth cannot be established with confidence but is conventionally given as 1620. Lombart studied graphic design under the great master Simon Vouet, but historians have been unable to determine where he learned the art of engraving, the skill for which he is chiefly remembered. The artist moved to England during the Cromwell era and earned his living as a engraver for several publishers. Although Lombart was neither as prolific nor as admired as Hollar, his fine frontispiece for Ogilby's Vergil was particularly well received. He died in Paris in 1681.

William Faithorne, born in London in 1616, was the only native Englishman among the Ogilby/Dryden artists. He studied under Robert Peake and fought for Charles I during the Civil War. Imprisoned after Charles was deposed, Faithorne was eventually released and lived in Paris until the Restoration. Upon returning to England, he established a printselling business, which he maintained for nearly thirty years. Best known for his portraits, many of them in color, Faithorne contributed only two plates to the *Aeneid*: "Aeneas and the Golden Bough" and "Aeneas Killing Turnus." He remained active as an artist until his death in 1691.

While Cleyn's drawings provided the basic designs for our *Aeneid* prints, Hollar, Lombart, and Faithorne were the actual printmakers. Hollar used a technique known as line etching whereas Lombart made engravings. Faithorne was skilled in both techniques and even wrote a celebrated book about engraving, but it is likely that he etched his *Aeneid* plates.

Both etching and engraving are *intaglio* processes, as are aquatint, mezzotint, and drypoint. In any intaglio process, the lines to be printed are cut into a metal (usually copper) sheet. Ink is then applied to the plate with a dabber, and the surface is wiped clean in such a way that the ink remains in the grooves. A piece of paper is placed on the plate, and together plate and paper are passed through a high-pressure roller press. The pressure is applied not so much to force the ink out of the grooves as to compress the paper at the uninked areas and to drive it into the grooves where it will receive the ink. Consequently, if you run your finger over a sheet printed by an *intaglio* process, you will feel that the inked areas of the paper are slightly raised.

An engraver actually carves into the plate using a tool called a burin, which cuts away the copper to form grooves for the ink. Because the burin has a diamond-shaped point, the deeper the cut, the wider the line will be. The engraver's burin is a difficult tool to use. It is held by a knob-shaped handle that fits comfortably into the palm. This grip gives the artist needed leverage but makes it difficult to control the direction of the cut. When a curved line is desired, the plate, not the burin, is turned.

An etcher makes grooves in the copper by an entirely different method. First, a protective "ground" is applied to the copper plate. This ground typically consists of "beeswax, asphaltum, pitch, and mastic in varying proportions according to the purpose for which they are intended."[1] Then a needle is used to scratch away the ground where the artist wants the lines to go. Next, the back and sides of the plate are varnished to protect them from damage. Finally, acid is poured on the plate. The acid eats away the exposed metal but does not harm the surfaces protected by the ground and varnish. At this point in the process, all of the grooves are of approximately the same depth. Those lines that are to remain shallow are "stopped out" by the application of varnish. The remaining lines can be deepened by the application of more acid, and the process can be repeated to produce as many different depths as the artist desires.

Although etched and engraved images may appear similar at first glance, there are subtle differences. Etched lines are more fluid, softer, less distinct, and have fuzzier edges. Engraved lines are sharper, bolder, and have crisp edges. Those with a practiced eye can differentiate between etched and engraved plates and, indeed, between Hollar's hand and Lombart's. Fortunately for those who have not yet developed such a skill, many of the *Aeneid* plates include attribution to Hollar, Lombart, or Faithorne. In these attributions, we read that Lombart always *"sculpsit"*

---

[1] Susan Lambert, *Prints: Art and Techniques* (London: V&A Publications, 2001) 55.

but Hollar and Faithorne always "*fecit*." There is a reason for the different verbs: The proper term for an engraver is "sculptor" because he actually carves the metal. The etcher, on the other hand, does not produce his lines by carving, so he is simply called an artist or "maker." It is important, however, not to rely exclusively on the attribution statements to identify the hands at work. It is likely that several of the plates engraved by Lombart also include sections etched by Hollar (typically the architectural details in the background), despite the lack of attribution.

From Ogilby to Dryden

Although John Dryden found Ogilby's Vergil translations to be entirely unsatisfactory, he seems to have had no such objections to the Ogilby illustrations, which his publisher, Jacob Tonson, had acquired from Thomas Guy. That Dryden knew of the illustrations is beyond doubt, and his contract with Tonson specified that plates should be printed with his translation "in Such manner and order as Shall be directed by the said Iohn Dryden."[2] The contract also stipulated that Tonson would have the responsibility to "amend Such of the Cutts as Shall want mending."[3] By the mid 1690s, however, all of the original artists were dead, so Tonson hired an unknown artist to retouch the plates and prepare them for use with the Dryden's new translation.

Side by side comparison of illustrations from the 1654 Ogilby and the 1697/8 Dryden reveals some significant differences. In Ogilby, the relevant Latin lines are inscribed below each illustration. In both works, each plate is accompanied by a dedication statement and coat of arms, but Dryden's dedicatees differ from Ogilby's. Because the Dryden editions would lack the Latin lines, Tonson instructed his engraver to add line numbers to the illustrations themselves. Keyed to the translation, these line numbers are often misleading, for the illustrations almost always incorporate details from an extended passage. The most striking change made by Tonson, however, was the alteration of Aeneas's appearance in most of the plates.

That the dedicatees would be different is hardly surprising. Dryden's Vergil was to be sold by subscription. Like the *Aeneid* itself, Dryden's work was eagerly anticipated and much discussed in literary circles even before its publication,[4] so finding subscribers was not likely to be problematic. Under Tonson's terms, the first 101 subscribers would pay five guineas — three in advance and two more upon receipt of the book.[5] In return, they would each receive a copy of the book. More importantly, Tonson would "cause to be engraved on the bottom of each plate the Name Title & Coat of Armes of each person Soe Subscribing."[6]

Dryden's contract with Tonson anticipated a second edition and allowed the poet to advertise for second subscriptions after he had completed *Aeneid* 6, his favorite book. By June of 1695, Dryden had reached that critical stage and was eager for the income that the second subscriptions would provide. He was to be paid only 200 pounds for the entire translation and had received only half that amount to date. He subsequently wrote to Tonson that if the second subscriptions did well, "I will take so much more time, because the profit will encourage me the more,"[7] especially since Dryden would get his cut up front this time. The second edition cost two guineas, one payable to Mr. Atterbury, Dryden's agent, at the time of subscription, and one to Tonson upon receipt of the book.

Because the actual cost of producing the book was far less than what subscribers paid, "subscription" was, in effect, a system of literary patronage. Like most patrons, the subscribers had motives that were not entirely altruistic, for to have one's name associated with Dryden's *Virgil* was a sign of cultural influence and prestige that could be

---

[2] *The Works of John Dryden*, ed. Frost and Dearing (Berkeley: University of California Press, 1987) 6.1180. Conventionally known as the "California Dryden," this work is hereafter abbreviated *CD*.

[3] *CD* 6.1180.

[4] See J. Barnard, "Early Expectations of Dryden's Translation of Virgil (1697) in England and on the Continent," *Review of English Studies* NS 50 (1999): 196–203.

[5] *CD* 6.1181.

[6] *CD* 6.1181.

[7] *The Letters of John Dryden*, ed. C. Ward (New York: AMS Press, 1965) 75.

exploited for political advantage. Although Tonson was contractually required to provide the subscribers, Dryden took an active role in the process, seeking subscriptions not only from his friends but also from those political figures whose views he supported.

When it came to politics, Dryden and Tonson did not see eye to eye. Dryden was a staunchly partisan Tory who had many friends in the court of Charles II. After Charles II died in 1685, his brother James II ascended the throne and undertook a variety of initiatives designed to convert England to Catholicism. Dryden himself converted. Then in 1688, William III, Prince of Orange and a descendant of Charles I, invaded England and eventually deposed James II to take the throne for himself and his wife Mary. In 1689, Dryden was stripped of his offices as poet laureate and historiographer royal. Not surprisingly, these developments displeased the poet, whose political connections were all but useless under the reign of William and Mary. Tonson, however, welcomed the changes, and it is in this political climate that he decided to have the Ogilby plates reworked so that Aeneas would resemble King William.

In changing the appearance of Aeneas, Tonson was hopeful that Dryden would dedicate his *Aeneid* to the king. Given the ancient ties between Aeneas and the emperor Augustus, Vergil's patron, such a dedication might have been apt, but Dryden wanted no part of it. On September 3, 1697, the poet wrote a letter to his sons in which he mocked Tonson's plans:

> But however he has missed of his design in the Dedication: though He had prepared the Book for it:
> for in every figure of Eneas, he has causd him to be drawn like K. William, with a hookd nose.[8]

To his publisher's evident displeasure, Dryden instead dedicated the *Aeneid* "To the Most Honourable John, Lord Marquess of Normanby, Earl of Mulgrave, &c. and Knight of the Most Noble Order of the Garter."

The final book that appeared in 1697 wasn't really a "book" at all but rather a collection of unbound leaves accompanied by a list of confusing and at times illogical assembly instructions. Subscribers and other recipients of the translation would have to take the leaves to a binder, but the quality of workmanship among late 17th century English binders was notoriously poor. Illiterate and often half-drunken or hung-over laborers would perform their task with appalling sloppiness. Errors in pagination and the gathering of signatures were not uncommon. Further, since the plates were printed on individual sheets already cut to size (as opposed to the folio leaves of the text), they had to be "tipped in," or inserted into an existing signature. This task was performed with equal carelessness. As a result, each of the 101 copies is a little different, with some plates either misplaced or completely missing.

The 1698 edition fared no better and perhaps a bit worse, for the addition of a list of second subscribers at the front of the book confused the pagination further. In all other respects, however, the second edition is identical to the first. Although there were also more copies of the second edition, the notion that "practice makes perfect" seems not to have applied.

The Bender Images

The images on the accompanying CD are, with two exceptions, taken from a copy of the 1698 Dryden edition in the collection of Henry Bender. The "Laocoon," which Dr. Bender's copy lacks, comes from the University of Pennsylvania's 1697 edition of Dryden. "The Trojan Horse," which is missing from both the Bender and Pennsylvania copies, comes from the Penn's 1654 edition of Ogilby's *Virgil*. All the images have a resolution of 96 dpi and are suitable for display on a computer screen, video monitor, or through an LCD projector.

David J. Califf, Ph.D.
The Academy of Notre Dame
Adjunct Professor of Classics, Villanova University

[8] *Letters* 93.

❧ Book I ❧

Discussion Questions

The questions provided below are designed to guide students through their study of the Dryden illustrations. Considering image and text in tandem serves several valuable goals. First, a careful examination of the illustrations will lead to a more thorough comprehension of the story of the *Aeneid*. In addition, the students' ability to recognize key Latin phrases at work in a given image will strengthen their skills in handling the Latin text. Finally, reflection on how the illustrator has *interpreted* the Latin text will enhance the students' literary critical acumen.

The first four questions below address the fundamental issues a reader of Vergil must confront when viewing each illustration. They are followed by supplementary questions that are specific to each image and draw attention to certain words and narrative details. Of course, teachers and students are encouraged to go far beyond these questions, which are conceived merely as discussion initiators.

General Questions:

1. In this illustration, where do you find a precise correspondence between the Latin text of Vergil and what is depicted?

2. Are there details in this illustration, which have no direct support in Vergil's Latin?

3. What probable identification(s) can be made between figure(s), detail(s), action(s), or setting(s) in this illustration and those directly or indirectly associated with Vergil's Latin?

4. In what ways can this image be considered as an interpretation of the artist rather than an illustration of the Latin text?

Vergil's *Aeneid*

The text supplied below includes all of the lines on the AP* Vergil syllabus. The italicized lines are those that inform specific illustrations in Dryden's translation. Some key phrases within the italicized lines receive emphasis by the illustrator; others do not. By considering how the illustrator has chosen to stress some textual details and exclude others, readers will acquire a heightened appreciation and more thorough understanding of each passage.

NO ILLUSTRATION FOR LINES 1–49

Arma virumque cano, Troiae qui primus ab oris
Italiam fato profugus Laviniaque venit
litora, multum ille et terris iactatus et alto
vi superum saevae memorem Iunonis ob iram;
multa quoque et bello passus, dum conderet urbem,   5
inferretque deos Latio, genus unde Latinum,
Albanique patres, atque altae moenia Romae.
Musa, mihi causas memora, quo numine laeso,
quidve dolens, regina deum tot volvere casus
insignem pietate virum, tot adire labores   10
impulerit. tantaene animis caelestibus irae?
    Urbs antiqua fuit, Tyrii tenuere coloni,
Karthago, Italiam contra Tiberinaque longe
ostia, dives opum studiisque asperrima belli;
quam Iuno fertur terris magis omnibus unam   15
posthabita coluisse Samo. hic illius arma,
hic currus fuit; hoc regnum dea gentibus esse,
si qua fata sinant, iam tum tenditque fovetque.
progeniem sed enim Troiano a sanguine duci
audierat, Tyrias olim quae verteret arces;   20
hinc populum late regem belloque superbum
venturum excidio Libyae; sic volvere Parcas.
Id metuens, veterisque memor Saturnia belli,
prima quod ad Troiam pro caris gesserat Argis —
necdum etiam causae irarum saevique dolores   25
exciderant animo; manet alta mente repostum
iudicium Paridis spretaeque iniuria formae,
et genus invisum, et rapti Ganymedis honores.
his accensa super, iactatos aequore toto
Troas, reliquias Danaum atque immitis Achilli,   30
arcebat longe Latio, multosque per annos
errabant, acti fatis, maria omnia circum.
Tantae molis erat Romanam condere gentem.
    Vix e conspectu Siculae telluris in altum
vela dabant laeti, et spumas salis aere ruebant,   35

cum Iuno, aeternum servans sub pectore vulnus,
haec secum: "mene incepto desistere victam,
nec posse Italia Teucrorum avertere regem?
quippe vetor fatis. Pallasne exurere classem
Argivum atque ipsos potuit submergere ponto,   40
unius ob noxam et furias Aiacis Oilei?
ipsa Iovis rapidum iaculata e nubibus ignem
disiecitque rates evertitque aequora ventis,
illum expirantem transfixo pectore flammas
turbine corripuit scopuloque infixit acuto;   45
ast ego, quae divum incedo regina, Iovisque
et soror et coniunx, una cum gente tot annos
bella gero! et quisquam numen Iunonis adorat
praeterea, aut supplex aris imponet honorem?"

Illustrations 1.1 a, b, c, d — The Storm (lines 50–131)

1. How is the presence of Juno made more dramatic than the text indicates?

2. What features of Aeolus correspond with his description in Latin?

3. How are the winds depicted in a manner that is not supported by the Latin text?

4. How does the Latin text inform the depiction of Aeneas, the oars, the sailors, and Neptune?

5. How faithful is the artist's rendering of the lightning, the scattering, and the loss of the other ships?

Write the answers to the questions in the space below.

ILLUSTRATION 1.1, THE STORM

Talia flammato secum dea corde volutans   *50*
nimborum in patriam, loca feta furentibus Austris,
Aeoliam venit. hic vasto rex Aeolus antro
luctantis ventos tempestatesque sonoras
imperio premit ac vinclis et carcere frenat.
illi indignantes magno cum murmure montis   *55*
circum claustra fremunt; celsa sedet Aeolus arce
sceptra tenens, mollitque animos et temperat iras.
ni faciat, maria ac terras caelumque profundum
quippe ferant rapidi secum verrantque per auras;
sed pater omnipotens speluncis abdidit atris,   *60*
hoc metuens, molemque et montis insuper altos
imposuit, regemque dedit, qui foedere certo
et premere et laxas sciret dare iussus habenas.
ad quem tum Iuno supplex his vocibus usa est:
  "Aeole, namque tibi divum pater atque hominum rex   *65*
et mulcere dedit fluctus et tollere vento,
gens inimica mihi Tyrrhenum navigat aequor,
Ilium in Italiam portans victosque Penates:
incute vim ventis submersasque obrue puppis,
aut age diversos et disiice corpora ponto.   *70*
sunt mihi bis septem praestanti corpore nymphae,
quarum quae forma pulcherrima Deiopea,
conubio iungam stabili propriamque dicabo,
omnis ut tecum meritis pro talibus annos
exigat, et pulchra faciat te prole parentem."   *75*
  Aeolus haec contra: "tuus, o regina, quid optes
explorare labor; mihi iussa capessere fas est.
tu mihi quodcumque hoc regni tu sceptra Iovemque
concilias, tu das epulis accumbere divum,
nimborumque facis tempestatumque potentem."   *80*
  Haec ubi dicta, cavum conversa cuspide montem
impulit in latus; ac venti, velut agmine facto,
qua data porta, ruunt et terras turbine perflant.
incubuere mari, totumque a sedibus imis
una Eurusque Notusque ruunt creberque procellis   *85*
Africus, et vastos volvunt ad litora fluctus.
insequitur clamorque virum stridorque rudentum.
eripiunt subito nubes caelumque diemque
Teucrorum ex oculis; ponto nox incubat atra.
intonuere poli et crebris micat ignibus aether   *90*
praesentemque viris intentant omnia mortem.
extemplo Aeneae solvuntur frigore membra:
ingemit, et duplicis tendens ad sidera palmas
talia voce refert: "o terque quaterque beati,
quis ante ora patrum Troiae sub moenibus altis   *95*
contigit oppetere! o Danaum fortissime gentis

ILLUSTRATIONS 1.1 A, B, C, D — THE STORM (1.50–131) [REPEATED]

1. How is the presence of Juno made more dramatic than the text indicates?

2. What features of Aeolus correspond with his description in Latin?

3. How are the winds depicted in a manner that is not supported by the Latin text?

4. How does the Latin text inform the depiction of Aeneas, the oars, the sailors, and Neptune?

5. How faithful is the artist's rendering of the lightning, the scattering, and the loss of the other ships?

    Write the answers to the questions in the space below.

Tydide! mene Iliacis occumbere campis
non potuisse, tuaque animam hanc effundere dextra,
saevus ubi Aeacidae telo iacet Hector, ubi ingens
Sarpedon, ubi tot Simois correpta sub undis   *100*
scuta virum galeasque et fortia corpora volvit?"
    Talia iactanti stridens Aquilone procella
velum adversa ferit, fluctusque ad sidera tollit.
franguntur remi, tum prora avertit, et undis
dat latus, insequitur cumulo praeruptus aquae mons.   *105*
hi summo in fluctu pendent; his unda dehiscens
terram inter fluctus aperit; furit aestus harenis.
tres Notus abreptas in saxa latentia torquet
(saxa vocant Itali mediis quae in fluctibus aras
dorsum immane mari summo); tres Eurus ab alto   *110*
in brevia et Syrtis urget, miserabile visu,
inliditque vadis atque aggere cingit harenae.
unam, quae Lycios fidumque vehebat Oronten,
ipsius ante oculos ingens a vertice pontus
in puppim ferit: excutitur pronusque magister   *115*
volvitur in caput, ast illam ter fluctus ibidem
torquet agens circum, et rapidus vorat aequore vertex.
apparent rari nantes in gurgite vasto,
arma virum tabulaeque et Troia gaza per undas.
iam validam Ilionei navem, iam fortis Achatae,   *120*
et qua vectus Abas, et qua grandaevus Aletes,
vicit hiems; laxis laterum compagibus omnes
accipiunt inimicum imbrem rimisque fatiscunt.
    Interea magno misceri murmure pontum,
emissamque hiemem sensit Neptunus, et imis   *125*
stagna refusa vadis, graviter commotus, et alto
prospiciens, summa placidum caput extulit unda.
disiectam Aeneae, toto videt aequore classem,
fluctibus oppressos Troas caelique ruina,
nec latuere doli fratrem Iunonis et irae.   *130*
Eurum ad se Zephyrumque vocat, dehinc talia fatur:

NO ILLUSTRATION FOR LINES 132–156

"Tantane vos generis tenuit fiducia vestri?   132
iam caelum terramque meo sine numine, venti,
miscere et tantas audetis tollere moles?
quos ego — sed motos praestat componere fluctus.
post mihi non simili poena commissa luetis.
maturate fugam regique haec dicite vestro:
non illi imperium pelagi saevumque tridentem,
sed mihi sorte datum. tenet ille immania saxa,
vestras, Eure, domos; illa se iactet in aula   140
Aeolus, et clauso ventorum carcere regnet."
    Sic ait et dicto citius tumida aequora placat
collectasque fugat nubes, solemque reducit.

Cymothoe simul et Triton adnixus acuto
detrudunt navis scopulo; levat ipse tridenti   145
et vastas aperit Syrtis et temperat aequor
atque rotis summas levibus perlabitur undas.
ac veluti magno in populo cum saepe coorta est
seditio, saevitque animis ignobile vulgus
iamque faces et saxa volant, furor arma ministrat;   150
tum, pietate gravem ac meritis si forte virum quem
conspexere, silent, arrectisque auribus adstant;
ille regit dictis animos, et pectora mulcet:
sic cunctus pelagi cecidit fragor, aequora postquam
prospiciens genitor caeloque invectus aperto
flectit equos curruque volans dat lora secundo.   156

ILLUSTRATIONS 1.2 A, B, C, D, E — LANDING AT THE HARBOR OF CARTHAGE (1.157–197)

1.   How does the port depicted in the scene conform to the Latin text?

2.   What is problematic about the depiction of the dead stags?

3.   What detail of the Latin text is curiously omitted from the illustration?

4.   What could be the motivation of the artist in making such an omission?

Write the answers to the questions in the space below.

Illustration 1.2, Landing at the Harbor of Carthage

Defessi Aeneadae quae proxima litora cursu
contendunt petere et Libyae vertuntur ad oras.
est in secessu longo locus: insula portum
efficit obiectu laterum, quibus omnis ab alto 160
frangitur inque sinus scindit sese unda reductos.
hinc atque hinc vastae rupes geminique minantur
in caelum scopuli, quorum sub vertice late
aequora tuta silent; tum silvis scaena coruscis
desuper horrentique atrum nemus imminet umbra. 165
fronte sub adversa scopulis pendentibus antrum,
intus aquae dulces vivoque sedilia saxo,
nympharum domus. hic fessas non vincula naves
ulla tenent, unco non alligat ancora morsu.
huc septem Aeneas collectis navibus omni 170
ex numero subit; ac magno telluris amore
egressi optata potiuntur Troes harena,
et sale tabentis artus in litore ponunt.
ac primum silici scintillam excudit Achates,
succepitque ignem foliis, atque arida circum 175
nutrimenta dedit, rapuitque in fomite flammam.
tum Cererem corruptam undis Cerealiaque arma
expediunt fessi rerum, frugesque receptas
et torrere parant flammis et frangere saxo.
　　Aeneas scopulum interea conscendit, et omnem 180
prospectum late pelago petit, Anthea si quem
iactatum vento videat Phrygiasque biremes,
aut Capyn aut celsis in puppibus arma Caici.
navem in conspectu nullam, tres litore cervos
prospicit errantis; hos tota armenta sequuntur 185
a tergo, et longum per vallis pascitur agmen.
constitit hic arcumque manu celerisque sagittas
corripuit, fidus quae tela gerebat Achates,
ductoresque ipsos primum, capita alta ferentis
cornibus arboreis sternit, tum vulgus et omnem 190
miscet agens telis nemora inter frondea turbam;
nec prius absistit, quam septem ingentia victor
corpora fundat humi, et numerum cum navibus aequet.
hinc portum petit, et socios partitur in omnis.
vina bonus quae deinde cadis onerarat Acestes 195
litore Trinacrio dederatque abeuntibus heros,
dividit, et dictis maerentia pectora mulcet:

No Illustration for Lines 198–222

"O socii (neque enim ignari sumus ante malorum),
o passi graviora, dabit deus his quoque finem.
vos et Scyllaeam rabiem penitusque sonantis 200
accestis scopulos, vos et Cyclopia saxa

experti: revocate animos, maestumque timorem
mittite; forsan et haec olim meminisse iuvabit.
per varios casus, per tot discrimina rerum
tendimus in Latium; sedes ubi fata quietas   205
ostendunt; illic fas regna resurgere Troiae.
durate, et vosmet rebus servate secundis."
          Talia voce refert, curisque ingentibus aeger
spem voltu simulat, premit altum corde dolorem.
illi se praedae accingunt dapibusque futuris: 210
tergora deripiunt costis et viscera nudant;
pars in frusta secant veribusque trementia figunt,
litore aena locant alii, flammasque ministrant.
tum victu revocant vires, fusique per herbam
implentur veteris Bacchi pinguisque ferinae.   215
postquam exempta fames epulis mensaeque remotae,
amissos longo socios sermone requirunt,
spemque metumque inter dubii, seu vivere credant
sive extrema pati nec iam exaudire vocatos.
praecipue pius Aeneas nunc acris Oronti,   220
nunc Amyci casum gemit et crudelia secum
fata Lyci, fortemque Gyan, fortemque Cloanthum.

ILLUSTRATIONS 1.3 A, B, C, D — VENUS, JUPITER, AND MERCURY (1.223–229, 297–301)

1. What precise moment in the narrative is enacted by this scene?

2. How does the illustrator assure the identification of each god depicted?

3. Why does Jupiter look away?

4. What detail of the Latin does not receive emphasis in the depiction of Venus?

5. Why is the image of Carthage dim?

6. In what way can this image of the gods as a group be interpreted as an illustrator's creative adaptation of the Vergilian poem?

Write the answers to the questions in the space below.

ILLUSTRATION 1.3, VENUS, JUPITER, AND MERCURY WITH CARTHAGE BELOW

Et iam finis erat, cum Iuppiter aethere summo
despiciens mare velivolum terrasque iacentis
litoraque et latos populos, sic vertice caeli   *225*
constitit et Libyae defixit lumina regnis.
atque illum talis iactantem pectore curas
tristior et lacrimis oculos suffusa nitentes
adloquitur Venus:

NO ILLUSTRATION FOR LINES 229–296

"O qui res hominumque deumque
aeternis regis imperiis, et fulmine terres,   230
quid meus Aeneas in te committere tantum,
quid Troes potuere, quibus tot funera passis,
cunctus ob Italiam terrarum clauditur orbis?
certe hinc Romanos olim volventibus annis,
hinc fore ductores, revocato a sanguine Teucri,   235
qui mare, qui terras omni dicione tenerent,
pollicitus — quae te, genitor, sententia vertit?
hoc equidem occasum Troiae tristisque ruinas
solabar, fatis contraria fata rependens;
nunc eadem fortuna viros tot casibus actos   240
insequitur. quem das finem, rex magne, laborum?
Antenor potuit mediis elapsus Achivis
Illyricos penetrare sinus atque intima tutus
regna Liburnorum, et fontem superare Timavi,
unde per ora novem vasto cum murmure montis   245
it mare proruptum et pelago premit arva sonanti.
hic tamen ille urbem Patavi sedesque locavit
Teucrorum, et genti nomen dedit armaque fixit
Troia; nunc placida compostus pace quiescit:
nos, tua progenies, caeli quibus adnuis arcem,   250
navibus (infandum!) amissis, unius ob iram
prodimur atque Italis longe disiungimur oris.
hic pietatis honos? sic nos in sceptra reponis?"
Olli subridens hominum sator atque deorum
vultu, quo caelum tempestatesque serenat,   255
oscula libavit natae, dehinc talia fatur:
"parce metu, Cytherea: manent immota tuorum
fata tibi; cernes urbem et promissa Lavini
moenia, sublimemque feres ad sidera caeli
magnanimum Aenean; neque me sententia vertit.   260
hic tibi (fabor enim, quando haec te cura remordet,
longius et volvens fatorum arcana movebo)
bellum ingens geret Italia, populosque ferocis
contundet, moresque viris et moenia ponet,
tertia dum Latio regnantem viderit aestas,   265
ternaque transierint Rutulis hiberna subactis.

ILLUSTRATIONS 1.3 A, B, C, D — VENUS, JUPITER, AND MERCURY (1.223–229, 297–301) [REPEATED]

1. What precise moment in the narrative does this scene enact?

2. How does the illustrator assure the identification of each god depicted?

3. Why does Jupiter look away?

4. What detail of the Latin does not receive emphasis in the depiction of Venus?

5. Why is the image of Carthage dim?

6. In what way can this image of the gods as a group be interpreted as an illustrator's creative adaptation of the Vergilian poem?

Write the answers to the questions in the space below.

at puer Ascanius, cui nunc cognomen Iulo
additur (Ilus erat, dum res stetit Ilia regno),
triginta magnos volvendis mensibus orbis
imperio explebit, regnumque ab sede Lavini 270
transferet, et longam multa vi muniet Albam.
hic iam ter centum totos regnabitur annos
gente sub Hectorea, donec regina sacerdos,
Marte gravis, geminam partu dabit Ilia prolem.
inde lupae fulvo nutricis tegmine laetus 275
Romulus excipiet gentem, et Mavortia condet
moenia, Romanosque suo de nomine dicet.
his ego nec metas rerum nec tempora pono:
imperium sine fine dedi. quin aspera Iuno,
quae mare nunc terrasque metu caelumque fatigat, 280
consilia in melius referet, mecumque fovebit
Romanos rerum dominos gentemque togatam;
sic placitum. veniet lustris labentibus aetas,
cum domus Assaraci Phthiam clarasque Mycenas
servitio premet ac victis dominabitur Argis. 285
nascetur pulchra Troianus origine Caesar,
imperium Oceano, famam qui terminet astris,
Iulius, a magno demissum nomen Iulo.
hunc tu olim caelo spoliis Orientis onustum
accipies secura; vocabitur hic quoque votis. 290
aspera tum positis mitescent saecula bellis;
cana Fides et Vesta, Remo cum fratre Quirinus,
iura dabunt; dirae ferro et compagibus artis
claudentur Belli portae; Furor impius intus,
saeva sedens super arma, et centum vinctus aenis 295
post tergum nodis, fremet horridus ore cruento."

Haec ait, et Maia genitum demittit ab alto
ut terrae utque novae pateant Karthaginis arces
hospitio Teucris, ne fati nescia Dido
finibus arceret. volat ille per aera magnum *300*
remigio alarum ac Libyae citus astitit oris.

NO ILLUSTRATION FOR LINES 302–304

Et iam iussa facit ponuntque ferocia Poeni 302
corda volente deo; in primis regina quietum
accipit in Teucros animum mentemque benignam. 304

Illustrations 1.4 a, b, c, d, e — Aeneas and Achates Meet the Disguised Venus (1.305–342, 365–8)

1.   What precise moment in the narrative does this scene enact?

2.   How has the illustrator paid very close attention to the Latin description of Aeneas?

3.   What Latin phrase describes the setting of this scene?

4.   How has the illustrator paid very close attention to the Latin description of the disguised Venus?

5.   How has the artist been strongly influenced by line 325?

6.   How does the scene reflect lines 365–368?

Write the answers to the questions in the space below.

ILLUSTRATION 1.4, AENEAS AND ACHATES MEET THE DISGUISED VENUS

At pius Aeneas per noctem plurima volvens,   *305*
ut primum lux alma data est, exire locosque
explorare novos, quas vento accesserit oras,
qui teneant (nam inculta videt) hominesne feraene,
quaerere constituit, sociisque exacta referre.
classem in convexo nemorum sub rupe cavata   *310*
arboribus clausam circum atque horrentibus umbris
occulit; ipse uno graditur comitatus Achate
bina manu lato crispans hastilia ferro.
    Cui mater media sese tulit obvia silva
virginis os habitumque gerens et virginis arma   *315*
Spartanae, vel qualis equos Threissa fatigat
Harpalyce volucremque fuga praevertitur Hebrum.
namque umeris de more habilem suspenderat arcum
venatrix dederatque comam diffundere ventis,
nuda genu, nodoque sinus collecta fluentis.   *320*
ac prior, "Heus," inquit, "iuvenes, monstrate mearum
vidistis si quam hic errantem forte sororum
succinctam pharetra et maculosae tegmine lyncis
aut spumantis apri cursum clamore prementem."
    Sic Venus; et Veneris contra sic filius orsus: *325*
"nulla tuarum audita mihi neque visa sororum,
o quam te memorem, virgo? namque haud tibi vultus
mortalis, nec vox hominem sonat; o, dea certe
(an Phoebi soror? an nympharum sanguinis una?),
sis felix nostrumque leves, quaecumque, laborem   *330*
et, quo sub caelo tandem, quibus orbis in oris
iactemur, doceas. ignari hominumque locorumque
erramus vento huc vastis et fluctibus acti:
multa tibi ante aras nostra cadet hostia dextra."
    Tum Venus: "haud equidem tali me dignor honore;   *335*
virginibus Tyriis mos est gestare pharetram
purpureoque alte suras vincire cothurno.
Punica regna vides, Tyrios et Agenoris urbem;
sed fines Libyci, genus intractabile bello.
imperium Dido Tyria regit urbe profecta,   *340*
germanum fugiens. longa est iniuria, longae
ambages; sed summa sequar fastigia rerum.

NO ILLUSTRATION FOR LINES 343–364

Huic coniunx Sychaeus erat, ditissimus agri
Phoenicum, et magno miserae dilectus amore,
cui pater intactam dederat, primisque iugarat   345
ominibus. sed regna Tyri germanus habebat
Pygmalion, scelere ante alios immanior omnis.
quos inter medius venit furor. ille Sychaeum
impius ante aras atque auri caecus amore,

clam ferro incautum superat, securus amorum   350
germanae; factumque diu celavit et aegram
multa malus simulans, vana spe lusit amantem.
ipsa sed in somnis inhumati venit imago
coniugis, ora modis attollens pallida miris,
crudelis aras traiectaque pectora ferro   355
nudavit, caecumque domus scelus omne retexit.
tum celerare fugam patriaque excedere suadet
auxiliumque viae veteres tellure recludit
thesauros, ignotum argenti pondus et auri.
his commota fugam Dido sociosque parabat.   360
conveniunt, quibus aut odium crudele tyranni
aut metus acer erat; naves, quae forte paratae,
corripiunt onerantque auro. portantur avari
Pygmalionis opes pelago; dux femina facti.

Devenere locos, ubi nunc ingentia cernes   365
moenia surgentemque novae Karthaginis arcem,
mercatique solum, facti de nomine Byrsam,
taurino quantum possent circumdare tergo.

NO ILLUSTRATION FOR LINES 369–452

   Sed vos qui tandem? quibus aut venistis ab oris?
quove tenetis iter?" quaerenti talibus ille   370
suspirans imoque trahens a pectore vocem:
   "O dea, si prima repetens ab origine pergam,
et vacet annalis nostrorum audire laborum,
ante diem clauso componet Vesper Olympo.
nos Troia antiqua, si vestras forte per auris   375
Troiae nomen iit, diversa per aequora vectos
forte sua Libycis tempestas appulit oris.
sum pius Aeneas, raptos qui ex hoste Penates
classe veho mecum, fama super aethera notus.
Italiam quaero patriam et genus ab Iove summo.   380
bis denis Phrygium conscendi navibus aequor,
matre dea monstrante viam, data fata secutus;
vix septem convulsae undis Euroque supersunt.
ipse ignotus, egens, Libyae deserta peragro,
Europa atque Asia pulsus." nec plura querentem   385
passa Venus medio sic interfata dolore est:
   "Quisquis es, haud, credo, invisus caelestibus auras
vitalis carpis, Tyriam qui adveneris urbem.
perge modo, atque hinc te reginae ad limina perfer.
namque tibi reduces socios classemque relatam   390
nuntio et in tutum versis aquilonibus actam,
ni frustra augurium vani docuere parentes.
aspice bis senos laetantes agmine cycnos,
aetheria quos lapsa plaga Iovis ales aperto
turbabat caelo; nunc terras ordine longo   395

aut capere aut captas iam despectare videntur:
ut reduces illi ludunt stridentibus alis
et coetu cinxere polum cantusque dedere,
haud aliter puppesque tuae pubesque tuorum
aut portum tenet aut pleno subit ostia velo.   400
perge modo et, qua te ducit via, dirige gressum."
    Dixit, et avertens rosea cervice refulsit,
ambrosiaeque comae divinum vertice odorem
spiravere; pedes vestis defluxit ad imos,
et vera incessu patuit dea. ille ubi matrem   405
agnovit, tali fugientem est voce secutus:
"quid natum totiens, crudelis tu quoque, falsis
ludis imaginibus? cur dextrae iungere dextram
non datur ac veras audire et reddere voces?"
talibus incusat gressumque ad moenia tendit.   410
at Venus obscuro gradientes aere saepsit
et multo nebulae circum dea fudit amictu,
cernere ne quis eos neu quis contingere posset
molirive moram aut veniendi poscere causas.
ipsa Paphum sublimis abit, sedesque revisit   415
laeta suas, ubi templum illi, centumque Sabaeo
ture calent arae sertisque recentibus halant.
    Corripuere viam interea, qua semita monstrat.
iamque ascendebant collem, qui plurimus urbi
imminet, adversasque adspectat desuper arces.   420
miratur molem Aeneas, magalia quondam,
miratur portas strepitumque et strata viarum.
instant ardentes Tyrii pars ducere muros,
molirique arcem et manibus subvolvere saxa,
pars optare locum tecto et concludere sulco.   425
iura magistratusque legunt sanctumque senatum.
hic portus alii effodiunt; hic alta theatris
fundamenta locant alii, immanisque columnas
rupibus excidunt, scaenis decora alta futuris.
qualis apes aestate nova per florea rura   430
exercet sub sole labor, cum gentis adultos
educunt fetus, aut cum liquentia mella
stipant et dulci distendunt nectare cellas,
aut onera accipiunt venientum, aut agmine facto
ignavum fucos pecus a praesepibus arcent;   435
fervet opus, redolentque thymo fragrantia mella.
"o fortunati, quorum iam moenia surgunt!"
Aeneas ait et fastigia suspicit urbis.
infert se saeptus nebula — mirabile dictu —
per medios, miscetque viris, neque cernitur ulli.   440
    Lucus in urbe fuit media, laetissimus umbrae,
quo primum iactati undis et turbine Poeni
effodere loco signum, quod regia Iuno
monstrarat, caput acris equi; sic nam fore bello
egregiam et facilem victu per saecula gentem.   445

hic templum Iunoni ingens Sidonia Dido
condebat, donis opulentum et numine divae,
aerea cui gradibus surgebant limina nexaeque
aere trabes, foribus cardo stridebat aenis.
hoc primum in luco nova res oblata timorem   450
leniit, hic primum Aeneas sperare salutem
ausus et adflictis melius confidere rebus.

ILLUSTRATIONS 1.5 A, B, C, D — AENEAS MEETS DIDO IN THE TEMPLE OF JUNO (1.453–519)

1. How has the illustrator interpreted line 456?

2. What characters in lines 458–493 can be securely identified in this illustration and why?

3. Offer plausible identifications for the other figures mentioned in lines 458–493.

4. What details and/or personages are omitted from the illustration and why?

5. Why does the figure of Juno receive central focus?

Write the answers to the questions in the space below.

Illustration 1.5, Aeneas Meets Dido in the Temple of Juno

Namque sub ingenti lustrat dum singula templo,
reginam opperiens, dum quae fortuna sit urbi
artificumque manus inter se operumque laborem   455
miratur, videt Iliacas ex ordine pugnas,
bellaque iam fama totum vulgata per orbem,
Atridas Priamumque et saevum ambobus Achillem.
constitit et lacrimans, "quis iam locus," inquit, "Achate,
quae regio in terris nostri non plena laboris?   460
en Priamus! sunt hic etiam sua praemia laudi,
sunt lacrimae rerum et mentem mortalia tangunt.
solve metus; feret haec aliquam tibi fama salutem."
sic ait atque animum pictura pascit inani,
multa gemens largoque umectat flumine vultum.   465
namque videbat uti bellantes Pergama circum
hac fugerent Graii, premeret Troiana iuventus;
hac Phryges, instaret curru cristatus Achilles.
nec procul hinc Rhesi niveis tentoria velis
agnoscit lacrimans, primo quae prodita somno   470
Tydides multa vastabat caede cruentus,
ardentesque avertit equos in castra prius quam
pabula gustassent Troiae Xanthumque bibissent.
parte alia fugiens amissis Troilus armis,
infelix puer atque impar congressus Achilli,   475
fertur equis curruque haeret resupinus inani,
lora tenens tamen; huic cervixque comaeque trahuntur
per terram et versa pulvis inscribitur hasta.
interea ad templum non aequae Palladis ibant
crinibus Iliades passis peplumque ferebant   480
suppliciter, tristes et tunsae pectora palmis;
diva solo fixos oculos aversa tenebat.
ter circum Iliacos raptaverat Hectora muros
exanimumque auro corpus vendebat Achilles.
tum vero ingentem gemitum dat pectore ab imo,   485
ut spolia, ut currus, utque ipsum corpus amici,
tendentemque manus Priamum conspexit inermis.
se quoque principibus permixtum agnovit Achivis,
Eoasque acies et nigri Memnonis arma.
ducit Amazonidum lunatis agmina peltis   490
Penthesilea furens mediisque in milibus ardet,
aurea subnectens exsertae cingula mammae,
bellatrix, audetque viris concurrere virgo.

   Haec dum Dardanio Aeneae miranda videntur,
dum stupet obtutuque haeret defixus in uno,   495
regina ad templum, forma pulcherrima Dido,
incessit magna iuvenum stipante caterva.
qualis in Eurotae ripis aut per iuga Cynthi
exercet Diana choros, quam mille secutae
hinc atque hinc glomerantur Oreades; illa pharetram   500

fert umero, gradiensque deas supereminet omnis
    (Latonae tacitum pertemptant gaudia pectus):
talis erat Dido, talem se laeta ferebat
per medios, instans operi regnisque futuris.
tum foribus divae, media testudine templi,   *505*
saepta armis solioque alte subnixa resedit.
iura dabat legesque viris, operumque laborem
partibus aequabat iustis, aut sorte trahebat:
cum subito Aeneas concursu accedere magno
Anthea Sergestumque videt fortemque Cloanthum   *510*
Teucrorumque alios, ater quos aequore turbo
dispulerat penitusque alias avexerat oras.
obstipuit simul ipse, simul percussus Achates
laetitiaque metuque; avidi coniungere dextras
ardebant, sed res animos incognita turbat.   *515*
dissimulant et nube cava speculantur amicti
quae fortuna viris, classem quo litore linquant,
quid veniant; cunctis nam lecti navibus ibant
orantes veniam et templum clamore petebant.

ILLUSTRATIONS 2.1 A, B, C — THE TROJAN HORSE (2.13–39)

1.   What details, not described in the italicized text, allude to subsequent scenes in Book II?

2.   Find the island of Tenedos, the *Dorica castra*, and the *pars stupea*.

3.   How do lines 35–39 inform the scene?

    Write the answers to the questions in the space below.

❧ Book II ❧

NO ILLUSTRATION FOR LINES 1–12

Conticuere omnes intentique ora tenebant;   1
inde toro pater Aeneas sic orsus ab alto:
　　　"Infandum, regina, iubes renovare dolorem,
Troianas ut opes et lamentabile regnum
eruerint Danai, quaeque ipse miserrima vidi,   5
et quorum pars magna fui. quis talia fando
Myrmidonum Dolopumve aut duri miles Ulixi
temperet a lacrimis? et iam nox umida caelo
praecipitat suadentque cadentia sidera somnos.
sed si tantus amor casus cognoscere nostros   10
et breviter Troiae supremum audire laborem,
quamquam animus meminisse horret luctuque refugit,
incipiam.

ILLUSTRATION 2.1, THE TROJAN HORSE

　　　Fracti bello fatisque repulsi
ductores Danaum tot iam labentibus annis
instar montis equum divina Palladis arte   15
aedificant, sectaque intexunt abiete costas;
votum pro reditu simulant; ea fama vagatur.
huc delecta virum sortiti corpora furtim
includunt caeco lateri, penitusque cavernas
ingentis uterumque armato milite complent.   20
　　　Est in conspectu Tenedos, notissima fama
insula, dives opum, Priami dum regna manebant,
nunc tantum sinus et statio male fida carinis:
huc se provecti deserto in litore condunt;
nos abiisse rati et vento petiisse Mycenas.   25
ergo omnis longo solvit se Teucria luctu;
panduntur portae, iuvat ire et Dorica castra
desertosque videre locos litusque relictum.
hic Dolopum manus, hic saevus tendebat Achilles;
classibus hic locus, hic acie certare solebant.   30
pars stupet innuptae donum exitiale Minervae

et molem mirantur equi; primusque Thymoetes
duci intra muros hortatur et arce locari,
sive dolo seu iam Troiae sic fata ferebant.
at Capys, et quorum melior sententia menti,   *35*
aut pelago Danaum insidias suspectaque dona
praecipitare iubent, subiectisque urere flammis,
aut terebrare cavas uteri et temptare latebras.
scinditur incertum studia in contraria vulgus.

NO ILLUSTRATION FOR LINES 40–56

Primus ibi ante omnes magna comitante caterva   40
Laocoon ardens summa decurrit ab arce,
et procul: "o miseri, quae tanta insania, cives?
creditis avectos hostis? aut ulla putatis
dona carere dolis Danaum? sic notus Ulixes?
aut hoc inclusi ligno occultantur Achivi,   45
aut haec in nostros fabricata est machina muros
inspectura domos venturaque desuper urbi,
aut aliquis latet error; equo ne credite, Teucri.
quidquid id est, timeo Danaos et dona ferentis."
sic fatus, validis ingentem viribus hastam   50
in latus inque feri curvam compagibus alvum
contorsit: stetit illa tremens, uteroque recusso
insonuere cavae gemitumque dedere cavernae.
et, si fata deum, si mens non laeva fuisset,
impulerat ferro Argolicas foedare latebras,   55
Troiaque, nunc staret, Priamique arx alta maneres.

ILLUSTRATIONS 2.2 A, B, C — LAOCOON (2.199–202, 212–222))

1. What details of lines 199–202 appear in the illustration?
2. Which details of lines 212–222 are omitted and which do this scene emphasize?

Write the answers to the questions in the space below.

Illustration 2.2, Laocoon

Hic aliud maius miseris multoque tremendum
obicitur magis atque improvida pectora turbat. 200
Laocoon, ductus Neptuno sorte sacerdos,
sollemnis taurum ingentem mactabat ad aras.

No illustration for lines 203–212

Ecce autem gemini a Tenedo tranquilla per alta
(horresco referens) immensis orbibus angues
incumbunt pelago pariterque ad litora tendunt; 205
pectora quorum inter fluctus arrecta iubaeque
sanguineae superant undas, pars cetera pontum
pone legit, sinuatque immensa volumine terga.
fit sonitus spumante salo; iamque arva tenebant,
ardentisque oculos suffecti sanguine et igni 210
sibila lambebant linguis vibrantibus ora.
diffugimus visu exsangues.

Illi agmine certo
Laocoonta petunt; et primum parva duorum
corpora natorum serpens amplexus uterque 215
implicat et miseros morsu depascitur artus;
post ipsum auxilio subeuntem ac tela ferentem
corripiunt spirisque ligant ingentibus; et iam
bis medium amplexi, bis collo squamea circum
terga dati superant capite et cervicibus altis.
ille simul manibus tendit divellere nodos, 220
perfusus sanie vittas atroque veneno,
clamores simul horrendos ad sidera tollit:

No illustration for lines 223–259

Qualis mugitus, fugit cum saucius aram
taurus et incertam excussit cervice securim.
at gemini lapsu delubra ad summa dracones 225
effugiunt saevaeque petunt Tritonidis arcem,
sub pedibusque deae clipeique sub orbe teguntur.
tum vero tremefacta novus per pectora cunctis
insinuat pavor, et scelus expendisse merentem
Laocoonta ferunt, sacrum qui cuspide robur 230
laeserit, et tergo sceleratam intorserit hastam.
ducendum ad sedes simulacrum orandaque divae
numina conclamant.
dividimus muros et moenia pandimus urbis.
accingunt omnes operi, pedibusque rotarum 235
subiciunt lapsus, et stuppea vincula collo
intendunt: scandit fatalis machina muros
feta armis. pueri circum innuptaeque puellae

sacra canunt, funemque manu contingere gaudent.
illa subit, mediaeque minans inlabitur urbi.   240
o patria, o divum domus Ilium et incluta bello
moenia Dardanidum, quater ipso in limine portae
substitit, atque utero sonitum quater arma dedere;
instamus tamen immemores caecique furore
et monstrum infelix sacrata sistimus arce.   245
tunc etiam fatis aperit Cassandra futuris
ora dei iussu non umquam credita Teucris.
nos delubra deum miseri, quibus ultimus esset
ille dies, festa velamus fronde per urbem.
      Vertitur interea caelum et ruit Oceano nox,   250
involvens umbra magna terramque polumque
Myrmidonumque dolos; fusi per moenia Teucri
conticuere; sopor fessos complectitur artus.
et iam Argiva phalanx instructis navibus ibat
a Tenedo tacitae per amica silentia lunae   255
litora nota petens, flammas cum regia puppis
extulerat, fatisque deum defensus iniquis
inclusos utero Danaos et pinea furtim
laxat claustra Sinon.

ILLUSTRATIONS 2.3 A, B, C, D, E — TROY INVADED (2.259–267)

1. How does the artist respond to the Latin word *laeti* in line 260?

2. In line 262 how is *funem* rendered in the scene?

3. The violent confrontation in the lower part of this scene represents what subsequent events as described in lines 402–452 (not included in the AP syllabus)?

4. What characters from lines 402–406 can be identified in this illustration?

Write the answers to the questions in the space below.

ILLUSTRATION 2.3, TROY INVADED

> *Illos patefactus ad auras*
reddit equus, laetique cavo se robore promunt 260
Thessandrus Sthenelusque duces et dirus Ulixes,
demissum lapsi per funem, Acamasque Thoasque
Pelidesque Neoptolemus primusque Machaon
et Menelaus et ipse doli fabricator Epeos.
invadunt urbem somno vinoque sepultam; 265
caeduntur vigiles, portisque patentibus omnis
accipiunt socios atque agmina conscia iungunt.

NO ILLUSTRATION FOR LINES 268–297

Tempus erat quo prima quies mortalibus aegris
incipit et dono divum gratissima serpit.
in somnis, ecce, ante oculos maestissimus Hector 270
visus adesse mihi largosque effundere fletus,
raptatus bigis ut quondam, aterque cruento
pulvere perque pedes traiectus lora tumentes.
ei mihi, qualis erat, quantum mutatus ab illo
Hectore, qui redit exuvias indutus Achilli, 275
vel Danaum Phrygios iaculatus puppibus ignis;
squalentem barbam et concretos sanguine crinis
vulneraque illa gerens, quae circum plurima muros
accepit patrios. ultro flens ipse videbar
compellare virum et maestas expromere voces: 280
"o lux Dardaniae, spes o fidissima Teucrum,
quae tantae tenuere morae? quibus Hector ab oris
exspectate venis? ut te post multa tuorum
funera, post varios hominumque urbisque labores
defessi aspicimus! quae causa indigna serenos 285
foedavit vultus? aut cur haec volnera cerno?"
ille nihil, nec me quaerentem vana moratur,
sed graviter gemitus imo de pectore ducens,
"heu fuge, nate dea, teque his," ait, "eripe flammis.
hostis habet muros; ruit alto a culmine Troia. 290
sat patriae Priamoque datum: si Pergama dextra
defendi possent, etiam hac defensa fuissent.
sacra suosque tibi commendat Troia Penatis:
hos cape fatorum comites, his moenia quaere
magna, pererrato statues quae denique ponto." 295
sic ait et manibus vittas Vestamque potentem
aeternumque adytis effert penetralibus ignem.

NO ILLUSTRATION FOR LINES 469–482

Vestibulum ante ipsum primoque in limine Pyrrhus
exsultat telis et luce coruscus aëna;   470
qualis ubi in lucem coluber mala gramina pastus,
frigida sub terra tumidum quem bruma tegebat,
nunc, positis novus exuviis nitidusque iuventa,
lubrica convolvit sublato pectore terga
arduus ad solem, et linguis micat ore trisulcis.   475
una ingens Periphas et equorum agitator Achillis,
armiger Automedon, una omnis Scyria pubes
succedunt tecto, et flammas ad culmina iactant.
ipse inter primos correpta dura bipenni
limina perrumpit, postisque a cardine vellit   480
aeratos; iamque excisa trabe firma cavavit
robora, et ingentem lato dedit ore fenestram.

ILLUSTRATIONS 2.4 A, B, C, D, E — THE DEATH OF PRIAM (2.483–558)

1. In the elaborate description of Pyrrhus and his actions, what aspects of his deeds are omitted from the illustration and why?

2. Identify and connect with specific Latin words the fire, the laurel tree, Hecuba and her daughters, Polites, Priam, and Pyrrhus.

3. How has the artist dramatically demonstrated the impact of Pyrrhus' mortal blow without showing the sword's full penetration into the body of Priam?

4. Lines 550–558 contain several stunning details that are not found in the illustration. What are these details, and why might they have been omitted?

5. What details of lines 550–558 do receive representation in the illustration?

Write the answers to the questions in the space below.

Illustration 2.4, The Death of Priam

Apparet domus intus, et atria longa patescunt;
apparent Priami et veterum penetralia regum,
armatosque vident stantis in limine primo.   485
at domus interior gemitu miseroque tumultu
miscetur, penitusque cavae plangoribus aedes
femineis ululant; ferit aurea sidera clamor.
tum pavidae tectis matres ingentibus errant
amplexaeque tenent postis atque oscula figunt.   490
instat vi patria Pyrrhus; nec claustra nec ipsi
custodes sufferre valent; labat ariete crebro
ianua, et emoti procumbunt cardine postes.
fit via vi; rumpunt aditus, primosque trucidant
immissi Danai, et late loca milite complent.   495
non sic, aggeribus ruptis cum spumeus amnis
exiit, oppositasque evicit gurgite moles,
fertur in arva furens cumulo camposque per omnes
cum stabulis armenta trahit. vidi ipse furentem
caede Neoptolemum geminosque in limine Atridas;   500
vidi Hecubam centumque nurus Priamumque per aras
sanguine foedantem, quos ipse sacraverat, ignis.
quinquaginta illi thalami, spes tanta nepotum,
barbarico postes auro spoliisque superbi
procubuere; tenent Danai qua deficit ignis.   505
  Forsitan et Priami fuerint quae fata requiras.
urbis uti captae casum convulsaque vidit
limina tectorum et medium in penetralibus hostem,
arma diu senior desueta trementibus aevo
circumdat nequiquam umeris, et inutile ferrum   510
cingitur, ac densos fertur moriturus in hostis.
aedibus in mediis nudoque sub aetheris axe
ingens ara fuit iuxtaque veterrima laurus
incumbens arae atque umbra complexa Penatis.
hic Hecuba et natae nequiquam altaria circum,   515
praecipites atra ceu tempestate columbae,
condensae et divum amplexae simulacra sedebant.
ipsum autem sumptis Priamum iuvenalibus armis
ut vidit, "quae mens tam dira, miserrime coniunx,
impulit his cingi telis? aut quo ruis?" inquit;   520
"non tali auxilio nec defensoribus istis
tempus eget, non, si ipse meus nunc adforet Hector.
huc tandem concede; haec ara tuebitur omnis,
aut moriere simul." sic ore effata recepit
ad sese et sacra longaevum in sede locavit.   525
ecce autem elapsus Pyrrhi de caede Polites,
unus natorum Priami, per tela, per hostis
porticibus longis fugit et vacua atria lustrat
saucius. illum ardens infesto vulnere Pyrrhus

ILLUSTRATIONS 2.4 A, B, C, D, E — THE DEATH OF PRIAM (2.469–558) [REPEATED]

6. In the elaborate description of Pyrrhus and his actions, what aspects of his deeds are omitted from the illustration and why?

7. Identify and connect with specific Latin words the fire, the laurel tree, Hecuba and her daughters, Polites, Priam, and Pyrrhus.

8. How has the artist dramatically demonstrated the impact of Pyrrhus' mortal blow without showing the sword's full penetration into the body of Priam?

9. Lines 550–558 contain several stunning details which are not found in the illustration. What are these details, and why might they have been omitted?

10. What details of lines 550–558 do receive representation in the illustration?

Write the answers to the questions in the space below.

insequitur, iam iamque manu tenet et premit hasta. 530
ut tandem ante oculos evasit et ora parentum,
concidit, ac multo vitam cum sanguine fudit.
hic Priamus, quamquam in media iam morte tenetur,
non tamen abstinuit, nec voci iraeque pepercit:
"at tibi pro scelere," exclamat, "pro talibus ausis, 535
di, si qua est caelo pietas quae talia curet,
persolvant grates dignas et praemia reddant
debita, qui nati coram me cernere letum
fecisti et patrios foedasti funere vultus.
at non ille, satum quo te mentiris, Achilles 540
talis in hoste fuit Priamo; sed iura fidemque
supplicis erubuit, corpusque exsangue sepulchro
reddidit Hectoreum, meque in mea regna remisit."
sic fatus senior telumque imbelle sine ictu
coniecit, rauco quod protinus aere repulsum 545
e summo clipei nequiquam umbone pependit.
cui Pyrrhus: "referes ergo haec et nuntius ibis
Pelidae genitori. illi mea tristia facta
degeneremque Neoptolemum narrare memento.
nunc morere." hoc dicens altaria ad ipsa trementem 550
traxit et in multo lapsantem sanguine nati,
implicuitque comam laeva, dextraque coruscum
extulit, ac lateri capulo tenus abdidit ensem.
haec finis Priami fatorum, hic exitus illum
sorte tulit, Troiam incensam et prolapsa videntem 555
Pergama, tot quondam populis terrisque superbum
regnatorem Asiae. iacet ingens litore truncus,
avulsumque umeris caput et sine nomine corpus.

NO ILLUSTRATION FOR LINES 559–566

At me tum primum saevus circumstetit horror.
obstipui; subiit cari genitoris imago, 560
ut regem aequaevum crudeli vulnere vidi
vitam exhalantem, subiit deserta Creusa
et direpta domus, et parvi casus Iuli.
respicio, et quae sit me circum copia lustro.
deseruere omnes defessi, et corpora saltu 565
ad terram misere aut ignibus aegra dedere.

ILLUSTRATIONS 2.6 A, B, C, D — THE ESCAPE OF AENEAS, ANCHISES, ASCANIUS, AND CRESUA (2.735–804)

1. The escape begins in line 721, and Aeneas is carefully described as lifting up his father onto his back, holding the hand(s) of his son, and then seeing that his wife follows behind. The details of the burning city render urgency to this scene. How does the artist convey an awareness of Creusa's impending death?

2. What lines refer to the Penates, clutched by Anchises?

    Write the answers to the questions in the space below.

Illustration 2.6, The Escape of Aeneas, Anchises, Ascanius, and Creusa

Hic mihi nescio quod trepido male numen amicum   *735*
confusam eripuit mentem. namque avia cursu
dum sequor et nota excedo regione viarum,
heu, misero coniunx fatone erepta Creusa
substitit, erravitne via seu lassa resedit,
incertum; nec post oculis est reddita nostris.   *740*
nec prius amissam respexi animumve reflexi
quam tumulum antiquae Cereris sedemque sacratam
venimus: hic demum collectis omnibus una
defuit, et comites natumque virumque fefellit.
quem non incusavi amens hominumque deorumque,   *745*
aut quid in eversa vidi crudelius urbe?
Ascanium Anchisenque patrem Teucrosque Penatis
commendo sociis et curva valle recondo;
ipse urbem repeto et cingor fulgentibus armis.
stat casus renovare omnes omnemque reverti   *750*
per Troiam et rursus caput obiectare periclis.
principio muros obscuraque limina portae,
qua gressum extuleram, repeto et vestigia retro
observata sequor per noctem et lumine lustro.
horror ubique animo, simul ipsa silentia terrent.   *755*
inde domum, si forte pedem, si forte tulisset,
me refero: inruerant Danai et tectum omne tenebant.
ilicet ignis edax summa ad fastigia vento
volvitur; exsuperant flammae, furit aestus ad auras.
procedo et Priami sedes arcemque reviso;   *760*
et iam porticibus vacuis Iunonis asylo
custodes lecti Phoenix et dirus Ulixes
praedam adservabant. huc undique Troia gaza
incensis erepta adytis, mensaeque deorum
crateresque auro solidi, captivaque vestis   *765*
congeritur. pueri et pavidae longo ordine matres
stant circum.
ausus quin etiam voces iactare per umbram
implevi clamore vias, maestusque Creusam
nequiquam ingeminans iterumque iterumque vocavi.   *770*
quaerenti et tectis urbis sine fine ruenti
infelix simulacrum atque ipsius umbra Creusae
visa mihi ante oculos et nota maior imago.
obstipui, steteruntque comae et vox faucibus haesit.
tum sic adfari et curas his demere dictis: *775*
"quid tantum insano iuvat indulgere dolori,
o dulcis coniunx? non haec sine numine divum
eveniunt; nec te hinc comitem asportare Creusam
fas, aut ille sinit superi regnator Olympi.
longa tibi exsilia, et vastum maris aequor arandum,   *780*
et terram Hesperiam venies, ubi Lydius arva
inter opima virum leni fluit agmine Thybris.

illic res laetae regnumque et regia coniunx
parta tibi; lacrimas dilectae pelle Creusae.
non ego Myrmidonum sedes Dolopumve superbas   *785*
aspiciam, aut Graiis servitum matribus ibo,
Dardanis, et divae Veneris nurus.
sed me magna deum genetrix his detinet oris.
iamque vale, et nati serva communis amorem."
haec ubi dicta dedit, lacrimantem et multa volentem   *790*
dicere deseruit, tenuesque recessit in auras.
ter conatus ibi collo dare bracchia circum;
ter frustra comprensa manus effugit imago,
par levibus ventis volucrique simillima somno.
sic demum socios consumpta nocte reviso.   *795*
    Atque hic ingentem comitum adfluxisse novorum
invenio admirans numerum, matresque virosque,
collectam exsilio pubem, miserabile vulgus.
undique convenere animis opibusque parati
in quascumque velim pelago deducere terras.   *800*
iamque iugis summae surgebat Lucifer Idae
ducebatque diem, Danaique obsessa tenebant
limina portarum, nec spes opis ulla dabatur.
cessi et sublato montes genitore petivi.

ILLUSTRATIONS 4.1 A, B — ANNA AND DIDO (4.1–55)

1. Which of the two figures is Dido and why? Support with references to the Latin.

2. Which of the two figures is Anna and why? Support with references to the Latin.

3. How has Vergil's adjective *saucia* (line 1) informed the artist's rendering of the scene?

4. With what Latin lines does the image of the undisturbed bed connect?

5. How does the landscape in the upper part of the illustration reflect the text of Vergil?

6. What is the significance of the gestures of each figure?

Write the answers to the questions in the space below.

\sim BOOK IV \sim

ILLUSTRATION 4.1, ANNA AND DIDO

At regina gravi iamdudum saucia cura
vulnus alit venis, et caeco carpitur igni.
multa viri virtus animo, multusque recursat
gentis honos: haerent infixi pectore vultus
verbaque, nec placidam membris dat cura quietem.   5
postera Phoebea lustrabat lampade terras,
umentemque Aurora polo dimoverat umbram,
cum sic unanimam adloquitur male sana sororem:
"Anna soror, quae me suspensam insomnia terrent!
quis novus hic nostris successit sedibus hospes,   10
quem sese ore ferens, quam forti pectore et armis!
credo equidem, nec vana fides, genus esse deorum.
degeneres animos timor arguit: heu, quibus ille
iactatus fatis! quae bella exhausta canebat!
si mihi non animo fixum immotumque sederet,   15
ne cui me vinclo vellem sociare iugali,
postquam primus amor deceptam morte fefellit;
si non pertaesum thalami taedaeque fuisset,
huic uni forsan potui succumbere culpae.
Anna, fatebor enim, miseri post fata Sychaei   20
coniugis et sparsos fraterna caede Penates,
solus hic inflexit sensus, animumque labantem
impulit; agnosco veteris vestigia flammae.
sed mihi vel tellus optem prius ima dehiscat,
vel Pater omnipotens adigat me fulmine ad umbras,   25
pallentes umbras Erebi noctemque profundam,
ante, Pudor, quam te violo, aut tua iura resolvo.
ille meos, primus qui me sibi iunxit, amores
abstulit; ille habeat secum servetque sepulchro."
sic effata sinum lacrimis implevit obortis.   30
    Anna refert: "O luce magis dilecta sorori,
solane perpetua maerens carpere iuventa,
nec dulcis natos, Veneris nec praemia noris?
id cinerem aut Manis credis curare sepultos?
esto: aegram nulli quondam flexere mariti,   35
non Libyae, non ante Tyro; despectus Iarbas
ductoresque alii, quos Africa terra triumphis
dives alit: placitone etiam pugnabis amori?
nec venit in mentem, quorum consederis arvis?
hinc Gaetulae urbes, genus insuperabile bello,   40
et Numidae infreni cingunt et inhospita Syrtis;
hinc deserta siti regio, lateque furentes
Barcaei. quid bella Tyro surgentia dicam,

germanique minas?
dis equidem auspicibus reor et Iunone secunda   *45*
hunc cursum Iliacas vento tenuisse carinas.
quam tu urbem, soror, hanc cernes, quae surgere regna
coniugio tali! Teucrum comitantibus armis
Punica se quantis attollet gloria rebus!
tu modo posce deos veniam, sacrisque litatis   *50*
indulge hospitio, causasque innecte morandi,
dum pelago desaevit hiems et aquosus Orion,
quassataeque rates, dum non tractabile caelum."
his dictis incensum animum flammavit amore,
spemque dedit dubiae menti, solvitque pudorem.   *55*

ILLUSTRATIONS 4.2 A, B — THE SACRIFICES OF DIDO (4.56–64)

1.   How does the artist render lines 58–59?

2.   Vergil names four gods. How does the sculptor identify these gods?

3.   In what specific ways do lines 60–62 inform the illustration?

4.   In what specific ways do lines 63–64 inform the illustration?

5.   What details does the artist include that are not mentioned in the Latin text?

Write the answers to the questions in the space below.

Illustration 4.2, The Sacrifices of Dido

Principio delubra adeunt, pacemque per aras
exquirunt; mactant lectas de more bidentes
legiferae Cereri Phoeboque patrique Lyaeo,
Iunoni ante omnis, cui vincla iugalia curae.
ipsa, tenens dextra pateram, pulcherrima Dido   60
candentis vaccae media inter cornua fundit,
aut ante ora deum pinguis spatiatur ad aras,
instauratque diem donis, pecudumque reclusis
pectoribus inhians spirantia consulit exta.

No illustration for lines 65–128

Heu vatum ignarae mentes! quid vota furentem,   65
quid delubra iuvant? est mollis flamma medullas
interea, et tacitum vivit sub pectore vulnus.
uritur infelix Dido, totaque vagatur
urbe furens, qualis coniecta cerva sagitta,
quam procul incautam nemora inter Cresia fixit   70
pastor agens telis, liquitque volatile ferrum
nescius; illa fuga silvas saltusque peragrat
Dictaeos; haeret lateri letalis harundo.
nunc media Aenean secum per moenia ducit,
Sidoniasque ostentat opes urbemque paratam;   75
incipit effari, mediaque in voce resistit;
nunc eadem labente die convivia quaerit,
Iliacosque iterum demens audire labores
exposcit, pendetque iterum narrantis ab ore.
post, ubi digressi, lumenque obscura vicissim   80
luna premit suadentque cadentia sidera somnos,
sola domo maeret vacua, stratisque relictis
incubat, illum absens absentem auditque videtque,
aut gremio Ascanium, genitoris imagine capta,
detinet, infandum si fallere possit amorem.   85
non coeptae adsurgunt turres, non arma iuventus
exercet, portusve aut propugnacula bello
tuta parant; pendent opera interrupta, minaeque
murorum ingentes aequataque machina caelo.
quam simul ac tali persensit peste teneri   90
cara Iovis coniunx, nec famam obstare furori,
talibus adgreditur Venerem Saturnia dictis:
"egregiam vero laudem et spolia ampla refertis
tuque puerque tuus (magnum et memorabile numen)
una dolo divum si femina victa duorum est.   95
nec me adeo fallit veritam te moenia nostra
suspectas habuisse domos Karthaginis altae.
sed quis erit modus, aut quo nunc certamine tanto?
quin potius pacem aeternam pactosque hymenaeos
exercemus? habes, tota quod mente petisti: 100

ardet amans Dido, traxitque per ossa furorem.
communem hunc ergo populum paribusque regamus
auspiciis; liceat Phrygio servire marito,
dotalesque tuae Tyrios permittere dextrae."
    Olli (sensit enim simulata mente locutam,   105
quo regnum Italiae Libycas averteret oras)
sic contra est ingressa Venus: "quis talia demens
abnuat, aut tecum malit contendere bello?
si modo, quod memoras, factum fortuna sequatur.
sed fatis incerta feror, si Iuppiter unam   110
esse velit Tyriis urbem Troiaque profectis,
miscerive probet populos, aut foedera iungi.
tu coniunx tibi fas animum temptare precando.
perge; sequar." tum sic excepit regia Iuno:
"mecum erit iste labor: nunc qua ratione, quod instat   115
confieri possit, paucis — adverte — docebo.
venatum Aeneas unaque miserrima Dido
in nemus ire parant, ubi primos crastinus ortus
extulerit Titan, radiisque retexerit orbem.
his ego nigrantem commixta grandine nimbum,   120
dum trepidant alae, saltusque indagine cingunt,
desuper infundam, et tonitru caelum omne ciebo.
diffugient comites et nocte tegentur opaca:
speluncam Dido dux et Troianus eandem
devenient; adero et, tua si mihi certa voluntas,   125
conubio iungam stabili propriamque dicabo.
hic hymenaeus erit." Non adversata petenti
adnuit, atque dolis risit Cytherea repertis.

ILLUSTRATIONS 4.3 A, B, C — LADY RUMOR (129–197)

1. Two scenes comprise this illustration. Identify the scenes and explain the relationship between them.

2. How do lines 130–132 find expression in the illustration?

3. What connections can be made between the artist's rendition of Dido and the details of line 136–139?

4. How is the tenuous relationship between Aeneas and Dido prefigured by their gestures in this illustration?

5. How has the artist captured the details of the storm (160–164)?

6. In what way has the artist paid particularly close attention to Vergil's description of *Fama* (173–197)?

Write the answers to the questions in the space below.

ILLUSTRATION 4.3, LADY RUMOR, THE STORM IN THE HUNT, AENEAS AND DIDO AT THE CAVE

Oceanum interea surgens Aurora reliquit.
it portis iubare exorto delecta iuventus;   *130*
retia rara, plagae, lato venabula ferro,
Massylique ruunt equites et odora canum vis.
reginam thalamo cunctantem ad limina primi
Poenorum exspectant, ostroque insignis et auro
stat sonipes, ac frena ferox spumantia mandit.   *135*
tandem progreditur, magna stipante caterva,
Sidoniam picto chlamydem circumdata limbo;
cui pharetra ex auro, crines nodantur in aurum,
aurea purpuream subnectit fibula vestem.
nec non et Phrygii comites et laetus Iulus   *140*
incedunt. ipse ante alios pulcherrimus omnes
infert se socium Aeneas atque agmina iungit.
qualis ubi hibernam Lyciam Xanthique fluenta
deserit ac Delum maternam invisit Apollo,
instauratque choros, mixtique altaria circum   *145*
Cretesque Dryopesque fremunt pictique Agathyrsi;
ipse iugis Cynthi graditur, mollique fluentem
fronde premit crinem fingens atque implicat auro;
tela sonant umeris: haud illo segnior ibat
Aeneas; tantum egregio decus enitet ore.   *150*
postquam altos ventum in montes atque invia lustra,
ecce ferae saxi deiectae vertice caprae
decurrere iugis; alia de parte patentes
transmittunt cursu campos atque agmina cervi
pulverulenta fuga glomerant montesque relinquunt.   *155*
at puer Ascanius mediis in vallibus acri
gaudet equo, iamque hos cursu, iam praeterit illos,
spumantemque dari pecora inter inertia votis
optat aprum, aut fulvum descendere monte leonem.
    Interea magno misceri murmure caelum   *160*
incipit, insequitur commixta grandine nimbus,
et Tyrii comites passim et Troiana iuventus
Dardaniusque nepos Veneris diversa per agros
tecta metu petiere; ruunt de montibus amnes.
speluncam Dido dux et Troianus eandem   *165*
deveniunt: prima et Tellus et pronuba Iuno
dant signum; fulsere ignes et conscius aether
conubiis, summoque ulularunt vertice nymphae.
ille dies primus leti primusque malorum
causa fuit; neque enim specie famave movetur,   *170*
nec iam furtivum Dido meditatur amorem:
coniugium vocat; hoc praetexit nomine culpam.
    Extemplo Libyae magnas it Fama per urbes —
Fama, malum qua non aliud velocius ullum:
mobilitate viget, viresque adquirit eundo,   *175*

ILLUSTRATIONS 4.3 A, B, C — LADY RUMOR (129–197) [REPEATED]

1. Two scenes comprise this illustration. Identify the scenes and explain the relationship between them.

2. How do lines 130–132 find expression in the illustration?

3. What connections can be made between the artist's rendition of Dido and the details of lines 136–139?

4. How is the tenuous relationship between Aeneas and Dido prefigured by their gestures in this illustration?

5. How has the artist captured the details of the storm (160–164)?

6. In what way has the artist paid particularly close attention to Vergil's description of *Fama* (173–197)?

    Write the answers to the questions in the space below.

parva metu primo, mox sese attollit in auras,
ingrediturque solo et caput inter nubila condit.
illam Terra parens, ira inritata deorum,
extremam, ut perhibent, Coeo Enceladoque sororem
progenuit, pedibus celerem et pernicibus alis,   *180*
monstrum horrendum, ingens, cui quot sunt corpore plumae,
tot vigiles oculi subter — mirabile dictu! —
tot linguae, totidem ora sonant, tot subrigit aures.
nocte volat caeli medio terraeque per umbram,
stridens, nec dulci declinat lumina somno;   *185*
luce sedet custos aut summi culmine tecti,
turribus aut altis, et magnas territat urbes;
tam ficti pravique tenax, quam nuntia veri.
haec tum multiplici populos sermone replebat
gaudens, et pariter facta atque infecta canebat: *190*
venisse Aenean Troiano sanguine cretum,
cui se pulchra viro dignetur iungere Dido;
nunc hiemem inter se luxu, quam longa, fovere
regnorum immemores turpique cupidine captos.
haec passim dea foeda virum diffundit in ora.   *195*
protinus ad regem cursus detorquet Iarban
incenditque animum dictis atque aggerat iras.

NO ILLUSTRATION FOR LINES 198–238

Hic Hammone satus rapta Garamantide nympha
templa Iovi centum latis immania regnis,
centum aras posuit, vigilemque sacraverat ignem,   200
excubias divum aeternas, pecudumque cruore
pingue solum et variis florentia limina sertis.
isque amens animi et rumore accensus amaro
dicitur ante aras media inter numina divum
multa Iovem manibus supplex orasse supinis: 205
"Iuppiter omnipotens, cui nunc Maurusia pictis
gens epulata toris Lenaeum libat honorem,
aspicis haec, an te, genitor, cum fulmina torques,
nequiquam horremus, caecique in nubibus ignes
terrificant animos et inania murmura miscent?   210
femina, quae nostris errans in finibus urbem
exiguam pretio posuit, cui litus arandum
cuique loci leges dedimus, conubia nostra
reppulit ac dominum Aenean in regna recepit.
et nunc ille Paris cum semiviro comitatu,   215
Maeonia mentum mitra crinemque madentem
subnexus, rapto potitur: nos munera templis
quippe tuis ferimus, famamque fovemus inanem."
    Talibus orantem dictis arasque tenentem
audiit Omnipotens, oculosque ad moenia torsit   220
regia et oblitos famae melioris amantes.
tum sic Mercurium adloquitur ac talia mandat:

"Vade age, nate, voca Zephyros et labere pennis,
Dardaniumque ducem, Tyria Karthagine qui nunc
exspectat, fatisque datas non respicit urbes,   225
adloquere, et celeris defer mea dicta per auras.
non illum nobis genetrix pulcherrima talem
promisit, Graiumque ideo bis vindicat armis;
sed fore, qui gravidam imperiis belloque frementem
Italiam regeret, genus alto a sanguine Teucri   230
proderet, ac totum sub leges mitteret orbem.
si nulla accendit tantarum gloria rerum,
nec super ipse sua molitur laude laborem,
Ascanione pater Romanas invidet arces?
quid struit, aut qua spe inimica in gente moratur,   235
nec prolem Ausoniam et Lavinia respicit arva?
naviget! Haec summa est; hic nostri nuntius esto."
        Dixerat.

Illustrations 4.4 a, b — Mercury Visits Aeneas (238–295)

1. What attributes of the figure of Mercury are mentioned in the text and what attributes are not?

2. In what ways do lines 260–264 receive special attention in the illustration?

3. Support an identification of the figure to the right of Aeneas.

4. Who is the goddess depicted in the niche at the far right, and why is she there? What clues, if any, can be found in the text?

5. What is the artistic function of the architectural elements in the illustration, and what correspondence exists between them and the Latin text?

Write the answers to the questions in the space below.

Illustration 4.4, Mercury Visits Aeneas as he Builds Carthage

Ille patris magni parere parabat
imperio; et primum pedibus talaria nectit
aurea, quae sublimem alis sive aequora supra   *240*
seu terram rapido pariter cum flamine portant;
tum virgam capit: hac animas ille evocat Orco
pallentes, alias sub Tartara tristia mittit,
dat somnos adimitque, et lumina morte resignat.
illa fretus agit ventos et turbida tranat   *245*
nubila; iamque volans apicem et latera ardua cernit
Atlantis duri, caelum qui vertice fulcit,
Atlantis, cinctum adsidue cui nubibus atris
piniferum caput et vento pulsatur et imbri;
nix umeros infusa tegit; tum flumina mento   *250*
praecipitant senis, et glacie riget horrida barba.
hic primum paribus nitens Cyllenius alis
constitit; hinc toto praeceps se corpore ad undas
misit avi similis, quae circum litora, circum
piscosos scopulos humilis volat aequora iuxta.   *255*
haud aliter terras inter caelumque volabat,
litus harenosum Libyae ventosque secabat
materno veniens ab avo Cyllenia proles.
ut primum alatis tetigit magalia plantis,
Aenean fundantem arces ac tecta novantem   *260*
conspicit; atque illi stellatus iaspide fulva
ensis erat Tyrioque ardebat murice laena
demissa ex umeris, dives quae munera Dido
fecerat, et tenui telas discreverat auro.
continuo invadit: "tu nunc Karthaginis altae   *265*
fundamenta locas, pulchramque uxorius urbem
exstruis? heu regni rerumque oblite tuarum!
ipse deum tibi me claro demittit Olympo
regnator, caelum et terras qui numine torquet,
ipse haec ferre iubet celeres mandata per auras: *270*
quid struis, aut qua spe Libycis teris otia terris?
si te nulla movet tantarum gloria rerum
[nec super ipse tua moliris laude laborem]
Ascanium surgentem et spes heredis Iuli
respice, cui regnum Italiae Romanaque tellus   *275*
debetur." tali Cyllenius ore locutus
mortales visus medio sermone reliquit
et procul in tenuem ex oculis evanuit auram.
     At vero Aeneas aspectu obmutuit amens,
arrectaeque horrore comae et vox faucibus haesit.   *280*
ardet abire fuga dulcesque relinquere terras,
attonitus tanto monitu imperioque deorum.
heu quid agat? quo nunc reginam ambire furentem
audeat adfatu? quae prima exordia sumat?
atque animum nunc huc celerem, nunc dividit illuc,   *285*

in partesque rapit varias perque omnia versat.
haec alternanti potior sententia visa est:
Mnesthea Sergestumque vocat fortemque Serestum,
classem aptent taciti sociosque ad litora cogant,
arma parent et quae rebus sit causa novandis   *290*
dissimulent; sese interea, quando optima Dido
nesciat et tantos rumpi non speret amores,
temptaturum aditus et quae mollissima fandi
tempora, quis rebus dexter modus. ocius omnes
imperio laeti parent et iussa facessunt.   *295*

NO ILLUSTRATION FOR LINES 296–449

At regina dolos — quis fallere possit amantem? —
praesensit, motusque excepit prima futuros,
omnia tuta timens. eadem impia Fama furenti
detulit armari classem cursumque parari.
saevit inops animi totamque incensa per urbem   300
bacchatur, qualis commotis excita sacris
Thyias, ubi audito stimulant trieterica Baccho
orgia nocturnusque vocat clamore Cithaeron.
tandem his Aenean compellat vocibus ultro:
"dissimulare etiam sperasti, perfide, tantum   305
posse nefas, tacitusque mea decedere terra?
nec te noster amor, nec te data dextera quondam
nec moritura tenet crudeli funere Dido?
quin etiam hiberno moliris sidere classem
et mediis properas Aquilonibus ire per altum,   310
crudelis? quid, si non arva aliena domosque
ignotas peteres, et Troia antiqua maneret,
Troia per undosum peteretur classibus aequor?
mene fugis? per ego has lacrimas dextramque tuam te
(quando aliud mihi iam miserae nihil ipsa reliqui),   315
per conubia nostra, per inceptos hymenaeos,
si bene quid de te merui, fuit aut tibi quicquam
dulce meum, miserere domus labentis et istam,
oro, si quis adhuc precibus locus, exue mentem.
te propter Libycae gentes Nomadumque tyranni   320
odere, infensi Tyrii; te propter eundem
exstinctus pudor et, qua sola sidera adibam,
fama prior. cui me moribundam deseris, hospes
(hoc solum nomen quoniam de coniuge restat)?
quid moror? an mea Pygmalion dum moenia frater   325
destruat aut captam ducat Gaetulus Iarbas?
saltem si qua mihi de te suscepta fuisset
ante fugam suboles, si quis mihi parvulus aula
luderet Aeneas, qui te tamen ore referret,
non equidem omnino capta ac deserta viderer."   330
dixerat. ille Iovis monitis immota tenebat
lumina, et obnixus curam sub corde premebat.

tandem pauca refert: "ego te, quae plurima fando
enumerare vales, numquam, regina, negabo
promeritam, nec me meminisse pigebit Elissae   335
dum memor ipse mei, dum spiritus hos regit artus.
pro re pauca loquar. neque ego hanc abscondere furto
speravi (ne finge) fugam, nec coniugis umquam
praetendi taedas, aut haec in foedera veni.
me si fata meis paterentur ducere vitam   340
auspiciis et sponte mea componere curas,
urbem Troianam primum dulcisque meorum
reliquias colerem, Priami tecta alta manerent,
et recidiva manu posuissem Pergama victis.
sed nunc Italiam magnam Gryneus Apollo,   345
Italiam Lyciae iussere capessere sortes:
hic amor, haec patria est. si te Karthaginis arces
Phoenissam Libycaeque aspectus detinet urbis,
quae tandem Ausonia Teucros considere terra
invidia est? et nos fas extera quaerere regna.   350
me patris Anchisae, quotiens umentibus umbris
nox operit terras, quotiens astra ignea surgunt,
admonet in somnis et turbida terret imago;
me puer Ascanius capitisque iniuria cari,
quem regno Hesperiae fraudo et fatalibus arvis.   355
nunc etiam interpres divum, Iove missus ab ipso
(testor utrumque caput) celeres mandata per auras
detulit; ipse deum manifesto in lumine vidi
intrantem muros vocemque his auribus hausi.
desine meque tuis incendere teque querelis;   360
Italiam non sponte sequor."
    Talia dicentem iamdudum aversa tuetur,
huc illuc volvens oculos, totumque pererrat
luminibus tacitis et sic accensa profatur:
"nec tibi diva parens generis nec Dardanus auctor,   365
perfide, sed duris genuit te cautibus horrens
Caucasus Hyrcanaeque admorunt ubera tigres.
nam quid dissimulo aut quae me ad maiora reservo?
num fletu ingemuit nostro? num lumina flexit?
num lacrimas victus dedit aut miseratus amantem est? 370
quae quibus anteferam? iam iam nec maxima Iuno
nec Saturnius haec oculis pater aspicit aequis.
nusquam tuta fides. eiectum litore, egentem
excepi, et regni demens in parte locavi;
amissam classem, socios a morte reduxi.   375
heu furiis incensa feror! nunc augur Apollo,
nunc Lyciae sortes, nunc et Iove missus ab ipso
interpres divum fert horrida iussa per auras.
scilicet is superis labor est, ea cura quietos
sollicitat. neque te teneo neque dicta refello.   380
i, sequere Italiam ventis, pete regna per undas.
spero equidem mediis, si quid pia numina possunt,

supplicia hausurum scopulis et nomine Dido
saepe vocaturum. sequar atris ignibus absens
et, cum frigida mors anima seduxerit artus,   385
omnibus umbra locis adero. dabis, improbe, poenas.
audiam et haec Manes veniet mihi fama sub imos."
his medium dictis sermonem abrumpit et auras
aegra fugit seque ex oculis avertit et aufert,
linquens multa metu cunctantem et multa parantem   390
dicere. suscipiunt famulae conlapsaque membra
marmoreo referunt thalamo stratisque reponunt.

    At pius Aeneas, quamquam lenire dolentem
solando cupit et dictis avertere curas,
multa gemens magnoque animum labefactus amore   395
iussa tamen divum exsequitur classemque revisit.
tum vero Teucri incumbunt et litore celsas
deducunt toto naves. natat uncta carina,
frondentesque ferunt remos et robora silvis
infabricata, fugae studio.   400
migrantes cernas totaque ex urbe ruentes:
ac velut ingentem formicae farris acervum
cum populant hiemis memores tectoque reponunt,
it nigrum campis agmen praedamque per herbas
convectant calle angusto: pars grandia trudunt   405
obnixae frumenta umeris, pars agmina cogunt
castigantque moras; opere omnis semita fervet.
quis tibi tum, Dido, cernenti talia sensus,
quosve dabas gemitus, cum litora fervere late
prospiceres arce ex summa, totumque videres   410
misceri ante oculos tantis clamoribus aequor?
improbe Amor, quid non mortalia pectora cogis?
ire iterum in lacrimas, iterum temptare precando
cogitur et supplex animos summittere amori,
ne quid inexpertum frustra moritura relinquat.   415
    "Anna, vides toto properari litore circum:
undique convenere; vocat iam carbasus auras,
puppibus et laeti nautae imposuere coronas.
hunc ego si potui tantum sperare dolorem,
et perferre, soror, potero. miserae hoc tamen unum   420
exsequere, Anna, mihi; solam nam perfidus ille
te colere, arcanos etiam tibi credere sensus;
sola viri molles aditus et tempora noras.
i, soror, atque hostem supplex adfare superbum:
non ego cum Danais Troianam exscindere gentem   425
Aulide iuravi classemve ad Pergama misi,
nec patris Anchisae cineres manesve revelli,
cur mea dicta negat duras demittere in aures?
quo ruit? extremum hoc miserae det munus amanti:
exspectet facilemque fugam ventosque ferentes.   430
non iam coniugium antiquum, quod prodidit, oro,
nec pulcro ut Latio careat regnumque relinquat:

tempus inane peto, requiem spatiumque furori,
dum mea me victam doceat fortuna dolere.
extremam hanc oro veniam — miserere sororis —   435
quam mihi cum dederit cumulatam morte remittam."

    Talibus orabat, talesque miserrima fletus
fertque refertque soror; sed nullis ille movetur
fletibus aut voces ullas tractabilis audit;
fata obstant placidasque viri deus obstruit aures.   440
ac velut annoso validam cum robore quercum
Alpini Boreae nunc hinc nunc flatibus illinc
eruere inter se certant; it stridor, et altae
consternunt terram concusso stipite frondes;
ipsa haeret scopulis et quantum vertice ad auras   445
aetherias, tantum radice in Tartara tendit:
haud secus adsiduis hinc atque hinc vocibus heros
tunditur, et magno persentit pectore curas;
mens immota manet, lacrimae volvuntur inanes.

NO ILLUSTRATION FOR LINES 642–692

At trepida et coeptis immanibus effera Dido
sanguineam volvens aciem, maculisque trementes
interfusa genas et pallida morte futura,
interiora domus inrumpit limina et altos   645
conscendit furibunda rogos ensemque recludit
Dardanium, non hos quaesitum munus in usus.
hic, postquam Iliacas vestes notumque cubile
conspexit, paulum lacrimis et mente morata
incubuitque toro dixitque novissima verba: 650
"dulces exuviae, dum fata deusque sinebat,
accipite hanc animam, meque his exsolvite curis.
vixi et quem dederat cursum fortuna peregi,
et nunc magna mei sub terras ibit imago.
urbem praeclaram statui, mea moenia vidi,   655
ulta virum poenas inimico a fratre recepi,
felix, heu nimium felix, si litora tantum
numquam Dardaniae tetigissent nostra carinae."
dixit, et os impressa toro "moriemur inultae,
sed moriamur" ait. "sic, sic iuvat ire sub umbras.   660
hauriat hunc oculis ignem crudelis ab alto
Dardanus, et nostrae secum ferat omina mortis."
dixerat, atque illam media inter talia ferro
conlapsam aspiciunt comites, ensemque cruore
spumantem, sparsasque manus. it clamor ad alta   665
atria: concussam bacchatur Fama per urbem.
lamentis gemituque et femineo ululatu
tecta fremunt, resonat magnis plangoribus aether,
non aliter quam si immissis ruat hostibus omnis
Karthago aut antiqua Tyros, flammaeque furentes   670
culmina perque hominum volvantur perque deorum.

audiit exanimis trepidoque exterrita cursu
unguibus ora soror foedans et pectora pugnis
per medios ruit, ac morientem nomine clamat:
"hoc illud, germana, fuit? me fraude petebas?   675
hoc rogus iste mihi, hoc ignes araeque parabant?
quid primum deserta querar? comitemne sororem
sprevisti moriens? eadem me ad fata vocasses:
idem ambas ferro dolor atque eadem hora tulisset.
his etiam struxi manibus patriosque vocavi   680
voce deos, sic te ut posita, crudelis, abessem?
exstinxti te meque, soror, populumque patresque
Sidonios urbemque tuam. date vulnera lymphis
abluam et, extremus si quis super halitus errat,
ore legam." sic fata, gradus evaserat altos,   685
semianimemque sinu germanam amplexa fovebat
cum gemitu atque atros siccabat veste cruores.
illa graves oculos conata attollere rursus
deficit; infixum stridit sub pectore vulnus.
ter sese attollens cubitoque adnixa levavit,   690
ter revoluta toro est oculisque errantibus alto
quaesivit caelo lucem, ingemuitque reperta.

ILLUSTRATIONS 4.6 A, B — THE VISITATION OF IRIS (693–705)

1. Though the illustration refers specifically to lines 685–705, in what ways is it also informed by the speech of Anna (675–685)?

2. What is Anna doing, and with what Latin lines do her actions connect?

3. What details in the rendition of Dido find textual support?

4. How are the details of lines 700–702 made manifest in the illustration?

5. Scholars believe that some of the illustrations were made by both Lombart (an engraver) and Hollar (an etcher). Find evidence of two different hands at work in this illustration.

Write the answers to the questions in the space below.

Illustration 4.6, The Visitation of Iris

Tum Iuno omnipotens, longum miserata dolorem
difficilesque obitus Irim demisit Olympo
quae luctantem animam nexosque resolveret artus.   695
nam quia nec fato merita nec morte peribat,
sed misera ante diem subitoque accensa furore,
nondum illi flavum Proserpina vertice crinem
abstulerat Stygioque caput damnaverat Orco.
ergo Iris croceis per caelum roscida pennis,   700
mille trahens varios adverso sole colores,
devolat et supra caput adstitit: "hunc ego Diti
sacrum iussa fero teque isto corpore solvo."
sic ait et dextra crinem secat, omnis et una
dilapsus calor, atque in ventos vita recessit.   705

BOOK VI

NO ILLUSTRATION FOR LINES 1–41

Sic fatur lacrimans, classique immittit habenas
et tandem Euboicis Cumarum adlabitur oris.
obvertunt pelago proras; tum dente tenaci
ancora fundabat naves et litora curvae
praetexunt puppes. iuvenum manus emicat ardens   5
litus in Hesperium; quaerit pars semina flammae
abstrusa in venis silicis, pars densa ferarum
tecta rapit silvas inventaque flumina monstrat.
at pius Aeneas arces quibus altus Apollo
praesidet horrendaeque procul secreta Sibyllae,   10
antrum immane, petit, magnam cui mentem animumque
Delius inspirat vates, aperitque futura.
iam subeunt Triviae lucos atque aurea tecta.

      Daedalus, ut fama est, fugiens Minoia regna
praepetibus pennis ausus se credere caelo   15
insuetum per iter gelidas enavit ad Arctos,
Chalcidicaque levis tandem super astitit arce.
redditus his primum terris, tibi, Phoebe, sacravit
remigium alarum, posuitque immania templa.
in foribus letum Androgeo; tum pendere poenas   20
Cecropidae iussi — miserum! — septena quotannis
corpora natorum; stat ductis sortibus urna.
contra elata mari respondet Gnosia tellus:
hic crudelis amor tauri suppostaque furto
Pasiphae mixtumque genus prolesque biformis   25
Minotaurus inest, Veneris monimenta nefandae,
hic labor ille domus et inextricabilis error;
magnum reginae sed enim miseratus amorem
Daedalus ipse dolos tecti ambagesque resolvit,

ILLUSTRATIONS 6.1 A, B — AENEAS AND THE SIBYL (42–97)

1. Identify the four central figures. How, if at all, can the figure at the extreme left be accounted for on the basis of the Latin text?

2. What is the connection between the portrayal of the Sibyl and lines 77–80 of the Latin text?

3. Attempt to identify the five figures at the top of the illustration and the three figures in the niches in the middle of the illustration.

4. This illustration is arguably the most problematic rendering of an *Aeneid* scene encountered thus far. In what specific ways does the image depart from a literal reading of the Latin text? How might the illustration nevertheless be justified as a valid pictorial interpretation of Aeneas's encounter with the Sibyl?

Write the answers to the questions in the space below.

caeca regens filo vestigia. tu quoque magnam   30
partem opere in tanto, sineret dolor, Icare, haberes.
bis conatus erat casus effingere in auro,
bis patriae cecidere manus. quin protinus omnia
perlegerent oculis, ni iam praemissus Achates
adforet, atque una Phoebi Triviaeque sacerdos,   35
Deiphobe Glauci, fatur quae talia regi:
"non hoc ista sibi tempus spectacula poscit;
nunc grege de intacto septem mactare iuvencos
praestiterit, totidem lectas de more bidentes."
talibus adfata Aenean (nec sacra morantur   40
iussa viri) Teucros vocat alta in templa sacerdos.

ILLUSTRATION 6.1, AENEAS AND THE SIBYL

Excisum Euboicae latus ingens rupis in antrum,
quo lati ducunt aditus centum, ostia centum;
unde ruunt totidem voces, responsa Sibyllae.
ventum erat ad limen, cum virgo "poscere fata   *45*
tempus" ait; "deus, ecce, deus!" cui talia fanti
ante fores subito non vultus, non color unus,
non comptae mansere comae; sed pectus anhelum,
et rabie fera corda tument, maiorque videri,
nec mortale sonans, adflata est numine quando   *50*
iam propiore dei. "cessas in vota precesque,
Tros" ait "Aenea? cessas? neque enim ante dehiscent
attonitae magna ora domus." et talia fata
conticuit. gelidus Teucris per dura cucurrit
ossa tremor, funditque preces rex pectore ab imo: *55*
"Phoebe, graves Troiae semper miserate labores,
Dardana qui Paridis direxti tela manusque
corpus in Aeacidae, magnas obeuntia terras
tot maria intravi duce te penitusque repostas
Massylum gentes praetentaque Syrtibus arva: *60*
iam tandem Italiae fugientis prendimus oras.
hac Troiana tenus fuerit Fortuna secuta;
vos quoque Pergameae iam fas est parcere genti,
dique deaeque omnes quibus obstitit Ilium et ingens
gloria Dardaniae. tuque, o sanctissima vates,   *65*
praescia venturi, da (non indebita posco
regna meis fatis) Latio considere Teucros
errantisque deos agitataque numina Troiae.
tum Phoebo et Triviae solido de marmore templum
instituam festosque dies de nomine Phoebi.   *70*
te quoque magna manent regnis penetralia nostris:
hic ego namque tuas sortis arcanaque fata
dicta meae genti ponam, lectosque sacrabo,
alma, viros. foliis tantum ne carmina manda,
ne turbata volent rapidis ludibria ventis;   *75*
ipsa canas oro." finem dedit ore loquendi.

At Phoebi nondum patiens immanis in antro
bacchatur vates, magnum si pectore possit
excussisse deum; tanto magis ille fatigat
os rabidum, fera corda domans, fingitque premendo.   *80*
ostia iamque domus patuere ingentia centum
sponte sua, vatisque ferunt responsa per auras:
"o tandem magnis pelagi defuncte periclis
(sed terrae graviora manent), in regna Lavini
Dardanidae venient (mitte hanc de pectore curam),   *85*
sed non et venisse volent. bella, horrida bella,
et Thybrim multo spumantem sanguine cerno.
non Simois tibi nec Xanthus nec Dorica castra
defuerint; alius Latio iam partus Achilles,
natus et ipse dea; nec Teucris addita Iuno   *90*
usquam aberit, cum tu supplex in rebus egenis
quas gentis Italum aut quas non oraveris urbes!
causa mali tanti coniunx iterum hospita Teucris
externique iterum thalami.
tu ne cede malis, sed contra audentior ito,   *95*
qua tua te Fortuna sinet. via prima salutis
(quod minime reris) Graia pandetur ab urbe."

NO ILLUSTRATION FOR LINES 98–136

    Talibus ex adyto dictis Cumaea Sibylla
horrendas canit ambages antroque remugit,
obscuris vera involvens: ea frena furenti   100
concutit, et stimulos sub pectore vertit Apollo.
ut primum cessit furor et rabida ora quierunt,
incipit Aeneas heros: "non ulla laborum,
o virgo, nova mi facies inopinave surgit;
omnia praecepi atque animo mecum ante peregi.   105
unum oro: quando hic inferni ianua regis
dicitur et tenebrosa palus Acheronte refuso,
ire ad conspectum cari genitoris et ora
contingat; doceas iter et sacra ostia pandas.
illum ego per flammas et mille sequentia tela   110
eripui his umeris, medioque ex hoste recepi;
ille meum comitatus iter maria omnia mecum
atque omnes pelagique minas caelique ferebat,
invalidus, vires ultra sortemque senectae.
quin, ut te supplex peterem et tua limina adirem,   115
idem orans mandata dabat. gnatique patrisque,
alma, precor, miserere (potes namque omnia, nec te
nequiquam lucis Hecate praefecit Avernis),
si potuit Manes arcessere coniugis Orpheus
Threicia fretus cithara fidibusque canoris,   120
si fratrem Pollux alterna morte redemit,
itque reditque viam totiens. quid Thesea, magnum
quid memorem Alciden? et mi genus ab Iove summo."
    Talibus orabat dictis arasque tenebat,
cum sic orsa loqui vates: "Sate sanguine divum,   125
Tros Anchisiade, facilis descensus Averno:
noctes atque dies patet atri ianua Ditis;
sed revocare gradum superasque evadere ad auras,
hoc opus, hic labor est. pauci, quos aequus amavit
Iuppiter aut ardens evexit ad aethera virtus,   130
dis geniti potuere. tenent media omnia silvae,
Cocytusque sinu labens circumvenit atro.
quod si tantus amor menti, si tanta cupido est,
bis Stygios innare lacus, bis nigra videre
Tartara, et insano iuvat indulgere labori,   135
accipe quae peragenda prius.

ILLUSTRATIONS 6.2 A, B, C — THE GOLDEN BOUGH (136–148, 183–211)

1. How do lines 136–148 inform this illustration? Pay special attention to careful rendering of particular Latin words.

2. How is the imagery of lines 190–192 expressed in the illustration?

3. Where and how is the *diva parens* of line 197 represented by the artist?

4. How does line 201 receive expression in this image?

5. What illustrative detail alludes to an earlier scene?

6. How is the function of the Golden Bough visually foreshadowed?

    Write the answers to the questions in the space below.

ILLUSTRATIONS 6.3 A, B — THE FUNERAL OF MISENUS (162–182)

1. Identify Misenus. Tell what in the text leads you to your choice.

2. What figures prominent in the illustration are not specifically mentioned by Vergil?

3. How are the details of lines 166–167 captured in the illustration?

4. What details in the illustration draw upon lines 179–182 of the text?

Illustration 6.2, The Golden Bough

    Latet arbore opaca
aureus et foliis et lento vimine ramus,
Iunoni infernae dictus sacer; hunc tegit omnis
lucus, et obscuris claudunt convallibus umbrae.
sed non ante datur telluris operta subire,   *140*
auricomos quam quis decerpserit arbore fetus.
hoc sibi pulchra suum ferri Proserpina munus
instituit. primo avulso non deficit alter
aureus, et simili frondescit virga metallo.
ergo alte vestiga oculis et rite repertum   *145*
carpe manu; namque ipse volens facilisque sequetur,
si te fata vocant; aliter non viribus ullis
vincere, nec duro poteris convellere ferro.

No Illustration for Lines 149–162

Praeterea iacet exanimum tibi corpus amici
(heu nescis) totamque incestat funere classem,   150
dum consulta petis nostroque in limine pendes.
sedibus hunc refer ante suis et conde sepulchro.
duc nigras pecudes; ea prima piacula sunto.
sic demum lucos Stygis et regna invia vivis
aspicies." Dixit, pressoque obmutuit ore.   155
    Aeneas maesto defixus lumina vultu
ingreditur linquens antrum, caecosque volutat
eventus animo secum. cui fidus Achates
it comes et paribus curis vestigia figit.
multa inter sese vario sermone serebant,   160
quem socium exanimem vates, quod corpus humandum
diceret.

Illustration 6.3, The Funeral of Misenus

    Atque illi Misenum in litore sicco,
ut venere, vident indigna morte peremptum,
Misenum Aeoliden, quo non praestantior alter
aere ciere viros Martemque accendere cantu.   *165*
Hectoris hic magni fuerat comes, Hectora circum
et lituo pugnas insignis obibat et hasta.
postquam illum vita victor spoliavit Achilles,
Dardanio Aeneae sese fortissimus heros
addiderat socium, non inferiora secutus.   *170*
sed tum, forte cava dum personat aequora concha,
demens, et cantu vocat in certamina divos,
aemulus exceptum Triton, si credere dignum est,
inter saxa virum spumosa inmerserat unda.
ergo omnes magno circum clamore fremebant,   *175*
praecipue pius Aeneas. tum iussa Sibyllae,
haud mora, festinant flentes, aramque sepulchri

congerere arboribus caeloque educere certant.
itur in antiquam silvam, stabula alta ferarum;
procumbunt piceae, sonat icta securibus ilex   *180*
fraxineaeque trabes cuneis et fissile robur
scinditur, advolvunt ingentis montibus ornos.

ILLUSTRATIONS 6.2 A, B, C — THE GOLDEN BOUGH (136–148, 183–211) **[REPEATED]**

1. How do lines 136–148 inform this illustration? Pay special attention to careful rendering of particular Latin words.

2. How is the imagery of lines 190–192 expressed in the illustration?

3. Where and how is the *diva parens* of line 197 represented by the artist?

4. How does line 201 receive expression in this image?

5. What illustrative detail alludes to an earlier scene?

6. How is the function of the Golden Bough visually foreshadowed?

Write the answers to the questions in the space below.

Illustration 6.2, The Golden Bough, continued

Nec non Aeneas opera inter talia primus
hortatur socios paribusque accingitur armis.
atque haec ipse suo tristi cum corde volutat 185
aspectans silvam inmensam, et sic voce precatur:
"si nunc se nobis ille aureus arbore ramus
ostendat nemore in tanto! quando omnia vere
heu nimium de te vates, Misene, locuta est."
vix ea fatus erat, geminae cum forte columbae 190
ipsa sub ora viri caelo venere volantes,
et viridi sedere solo. tum maximus heros
maternas agnoscit aves laetusque precatur:
"este duces, o, si qua via est, cursumque per auras
dirigite in lucos, ubi pinguem dives opacat 195
ramus humum. tuque, o, dubiis ne defice rebus,
diva parens." sic effatus vestigia pressit
observans quae signa ferant, quo tendere pergant.
pascentes illae tantum prodire volando
quantum acie possent oculi servare sequentum. 200
inde ubi venere ad fauces grave olentis Averni,
tollunt se celeres liquidumque per aera lapsae
sedibus optatis gemina super arbore sidunt,
discolor unde auri per ramos aura refulsit.
quale solet silvis brumali frigore viscum 205
fronde virere nova, quod non sua seminat arbos,
et croceo fetu teretes circumdare truncos,
talis erat species auri frondentis opaca
ilice, sic leni crepitabat brattea vento.
corripit Aeneas extemplo avidusque refringit 210
cunctantem, et vatis portat sub tecta Sibyllae.

Illustrations 6.6 a, b, c — Aeneas Meets Dido in the Underworld (450–476)

1. Identify the four figures in the foreground. List the specific words in the text that support your choice.

2. Find details in the upper right that allude to earlier episodes in *Aeneid* 6.

3. The *quas* of line 450 refers to women that are rendered in the upper portion of this illustration. Based on a reading of lines 426–449 (not on the AP syllabus), what possible identifications can be made for those figures?

4. What precise moment does this scene illustrate?

5. What specific connections can be made between the Latin text and Dido's appearance, pose, and gestures in the illustration?

Write the answers to the questions in the space below.

ILLUSTRATION 6.6, AENEAS MEETS DIDO IN THE UNDERWORLD

Inter quas Phoenissa recens a vulnere Dido   *450*
errabat silva in magna; quam Troius heros
ut primum iuxta stetit agnovitque per umbras
obscuram, qualem primo qui surgere mense
aut videt, aut vidisse putat per nubila lunam,
demisit lacrimas dulcique adfatus amore est: *455*
"infelix Dido, verus mihi nuntius ergo
venerat exstinctam ferroque extrema secutam?
funeris heu tibi causa fui? per sidera iuro,
per superos, et si qua fides tellure sub ima est,
invitus, regina, tuo de litore cessi.   *460*
sed me iussa deum, quae nunc has ire per umbras,
per loca senta situ cogunt noctemque profundam,
imperiis egere suis; nec credere quivi
hunc tantum tibi me discessu ferre dolorem.
siste gradum teque aspectu ne subtrahe nostro.   *465*
quem fugis? extremum fato quod te adloquor hoc est."
talibus Aeneas ardentem et torva tuentem
lenibat dictis animum lacrimasque ciebat.
illa solo fixos oculos aversa tenebat
nec magis incepto vultum sermone movetur   *470*
quam si dura silex aut stet Marpesia cautes.
tandem corripuit sese atque inimica refugit
in nemus umbriferum, coniunx ubi pristinus illi
respondet curis aequatque Sychaeus amorem.
nec minus Aeneas casu concussus iniquo   *475*
prosequitur lacrimis longe et miseratur euntem.

ILLUSTRATION 6.8 A, B, C, D — THE PARADE OF HEROES (756–901, OF WHICH LINES 756–846 ARE NOT ON THE AP SYLLABUS)

1. Identify the three central figures. List the specific words in the text that support your choice.

2. The precise identification of the figures in the parade is problematic. Nevertheless, what tentative identifications can be made on the basis of the Latin text?

    Write the answers to the questions in the space below.

Illustration 6.8, The Parade of Heroes

"Excudent alii spirantia mollius aera
(credo equidem), vivos ducent de marmore vultus,
orabunt causas melius, caelique meatus
describent radio et surgentia sidera dicent: *850*
tu regere imperio populos, Romane, memento
(hae tibi erunt artes), pacisque imponere morem,
parcere subiectis, et debellare superbos."

    Sic pater Anchises, atque haec mirantibus addit:
"aspice, ut insignis spoliis Marcellus opimis   *855*
ingreditur, victorque viros supereminet omnes.
hic rem Romanam magno turbante tumultu
sistet eques, sternet Poenos Gallumque rebellem,
tertiaque arma patri suspendet capta Quirino."
atque hic Aeneas (una namque ire videbat   *860*
egregium forma iuvenem et fulgentibus armis,
sed frons laeta parum et deiecto lumina vultu):
"quis, pater, ille, virum qui sic comitatur euntem?
filius, anne aliquis magna de stirpe nepotum?
quis strepitus circa comitum! quantum instar in ipso!   *865*
sed nox atra caput tristi circumvolat umbra."
tum pater Anchises lacrimis ingressus obortis:
"o gnate, ingentem luctum ne quaere tuorum;
ostendent terris hunc tantum fata neque ultra
esse sinent. nimium vobis Romana propago   *870*
visa potens, superi, propria haec si dona fuissent.
quantos ille virum magnam Mavortis ad urbem
campus aget gemitus! vel quae, Tiberine, videbis
funera, cum tumulum praeterlabere recentem!
nec puer Iliaca quisquam de gente Latinos   *875*
in tantum spe tollet avos, nec Romula quondam
ullo se tantum tellus iactabit alumno.
heu pietas, heu prisca fides, invictaque bello
dextera! non illi se quisquam impune tulisset
obvius armato, seu cum pedes iret in hostem   *880*
seu spumantis equi foderet calcaribus armos.
heu, miserande puer, si qua fata aspera rumpas,
tu Marcellus eris. manibus date lilia plenis,
purpureos spargam flores animamque nepotis
his saltem accumulem donis, et fungar inani   *885*
munere." sic tota passim regione vagantur
aeris in campis latis atque omnia lustrant.
quae postquam Anchises natum per singula duxit
incenditque animum famae venientis amore,
exim bella viro memorat quae deinde gerenda,   *890*
Laurentesque docet populos urbemque Latini,
et quo quemque modo fugiatque feratque laborem.

    Sunt geminae Somni portae, quarum altera fertur
cornea, qua veris facilis datur exitus umbris,

> *altera candenti perfecta nitens elephanto,*   *895*
> *sed falsa ad caelum mittunt insomnia Manes.*
> *his ubi tum natum Anchises unaque Sibyllam*
> *prosequitur dictis, portaque emittit eburna;*
> *ille viam secat ad naves sociosque revisit.*
>   *Tum se ad Caietae recto fert litore portum.*   *900*
> *ancora de prora iacitur; stant litore puppes.*

ILLUSTRATIONS 10.3 A, B, C, D, E — TURNUS TAKES THE BELT OF PALLAS (420–473, 495–509)

1. Who are the figures in the foreground, and what character lies dead just behind them?

2. Identify the figures above the clouds with reference to their attributes. With appropriate citations from the text (464–472), justify the expression and gestures of the figure on the right.

3. What figure prominent in the narrative (432–439) does not have prominence in the illustration?

4. What is the impact of lines 439–40 on the scene?

5. What details from lines 495–509 are explicitly represented by the artist?

Write the answers to the questions in the space below.

❦ BOOK X ❦

ILLUSTRATION 10.3, TURNUS TAKES THE BELT OF PALLAS

Quem sic Pallas petit ante precatus: 420
       "Da nunc, Thybri pater, ferro, quod missile libro,
fortunam atque viam duri per pectus Halaesi.
haec arma exuviasque viri tua quercus habebit."
audiit illa deus; dum texit Imaona Halaesus,
Arcadio infelix telo dat pectus inermum.   425
at non caede viri tanta perterrita Lausus,
pars ingens belli, sinit agmina: primus Abantem
oppositum interimit, pugnae nodumque moramque.
sternitur Arcadiae proles, sternuntur Etrusci
et vos, o Grais imperdita corpora, Teucri.   430
agmina concurrunt ducibusque et viribus aequis;
extremi addensent acies nec turba moveri
tela manusque sinit. hinc Pallas instat et urget,
hinc contra Lausus, nec multum discrepat aetas,
egregii forma, sed quis Fortuna negarat   435
in patriam reditus. ipsos concurrere passus
haud tamen inter se magni regnator Olympi;
mox illos sua fata manent maiore sub hoste.
       Interea soror alma monet succedere Lauso
Turnum, qui volucri curru medium secat agmen.   440
ut vidit socios: "tempus desistere pugnae;
solus ego in Pallanta feror, soli mihi Pallas
debetur; cuperem ipse parens spectator adesset."
haec ait, et socii cesserunt aequore iusso.
at Rutulum abscessu iuvenis tum iussa superba   445
miratus stupet in Turno corpusque per ingens
lumina volvit obitque truci procul omnia visu,
talibus et dictis it contra dicta tyranni:
"aut spoliis ego iam raptis laudabor opimis
aut leto insigni: sorti pater aequus utrique est.   450
tolle minas." fatus medium procedit in aequor.
frigidus Arcadibus coit in praecordia sanguis.
desiluit Turnus biiugis, pedes apparat ire
comminus; utque leo, specula cum vidit ab alta
stare procul campis meditantem in proelia taurum,   455
advolat, haud alia est Turni venientis imago.
hunc ubi contiguum missae fore credidit hastae,
ire prior Pallas, siqua fors adiuvet ausum
viribus imparibus, magnumque ita ad aethera fatur:
"per patris hospitium et mensas, quas advena adisti,   460
te precor, Alcide, coeptis ingentibus adsis.
cernat semineci sibi me rapere arma cruenta

victoremque ferant morientia lumina Turni."
audiit Alcides iuvenem magnumque sub imo
corde premit gemitum lacrimasque effundit inanis.   *465*

ILLUSTRATIONS 10.3 A, B, C, D, E — TURNUS TAKES THE BELT OF PALLAS (420–472, 495–509) [REPEATED]

1. Who are the figures in the foreground, and what character lies dead just behind them?

2. Identify the figures above the clouds with reference to their attributes. With appropriate citations from the text (464–472), justify the expression and gestures of the figure on the right.

3. What figure prominent in the narrative (432–439) does not have prominence in the illustration?

4. What is the impact of lines 439–40 on the scene?

5. What details from lines 495–509 are explicitly represented by the artist?

Write the answers to the questions in the space below.

tum genitor natum dictis adfatur amicis:
"stat sua cuique dies, breve et inreparabile tempus
omnibus est vitae; sed famam extendere factis,
hoc virtutis opus. Troiae sub moenibus altis
tot gnati cecidere deum, quin occidit una   *470*
Sarpedon, mea progenies; etiam sua Turnum
fata vocant, metasque dati pervenit ad aevi."

NO ILLUSTRATION FOR LINES 473–495

Sic ait atque oculos Rutulorum reicit arvis.
at Pallas magnis emittit viribus hastam
vaginaque cava fulgentem deripit ensem.   475
illa volans umeri surgunt qua tegmina summa
incidit atque viam clipei molita per oras
tandem etiam magno strinxit de corpore Turni.
hic Turnus ferro praefixum robur acuto
in Pallanta diu librans iacit atque ita fatur: 480
"aspice num mage sit nostrum penetrabile telum."
dixerat; at clipeum, tot ferri terga, tot aeris,
quem pellis totiens obeat circumdata tauri,
vibranti cuspis medium transverberat ictu
loricaeque moras et pectus perforat ingens.   485
ille rapit calidum frustra de vulnere telum:
una eademque via sanguis animusque sequuntur.
corruit in vulnus (sonitum super arma dedere)
et terram hostilem moriens petit ore cruento.
quem Turnus super adsistens: 490
"Arcades, haec" inquit "memores mea dicta referte
Evandro: qualem meruit, Pallanta remitto.
quisquis honos tumuli, quidquid solamen humandi est,
largior. haud illi stabunt Aeneia parvo
hospitia."

   Et laevo pressit pede talia fatus   495
exanimem, rapiens immania pondera baltei
impressumque nefas: una sub nocte iugali
caesa manus iuvenum foede thalamique cruenti,
quae Clonus Eurytides multo caelaverat auro;
quo nunc Turnus ovat spolio gaudetque potitus.   500
nescia mens hominum fati sortisque futurae
et servare modum rebus sublata secundis!
Turno tempus erit magno cum optaverit emptum
intactum Pallanta, et cum spolia ista diemque
oderit. at socii multo gemitu lacrimisque   505
impositum scuto referunt Pallanta frequentes.
o dolor atque decus magnum rediture parenti,
haec te prima dies bello dedit, haec eadem aufert,
cum tamen ingentes Rutulorum linquis acervos!

Illustrations 12.4 a, b, c, d — Gods on Olympus (791–842), Aeneas Extracts Spear (766–790, not on the AP syllabus)

1. Why has the illustrator chosen to combine these two scenes in a single image?

2. Identify the heavenly figures based on their attributes.

3. What is the special effect of line 792 on the artist's conception of this scene?

Write the answers to the questions in the space below.

Book XII

ILLUSTRATION 12.4, THE GODS ON OLYMPUS

Iunonem interea rex omnipotentis Olympi
adloquitur fulva pugnas de nube tuentem:
"quae iam finis erit, coniunx? quid denique restat?
indigetem Aenean scis ipsa et scire fateris
deberi caelo fatisque ad sidera tolli.   795
quid struis? aut qua spe gelidis in nubibus haeres?
mortalin decuit violari vulnere divum?
aut ensem (quid enim sine te Iuturna valeret?)
creptum reddi Turno et vim crescere victis?
desine iam tandem precibusque inflectere nostris,   800
ne te tantus edit tacitam dolor et mihi curae
saepe tuo dulci tristes ex ore recursent.
ventum ad supremum est. terris agitare vel undis
Troianos potuisti, infandum accendere bellum,
deformare domum et luctu miscere hymenaeos: 805
ulterius temptare veto." sic Iuppiter orsus;
sic dea submisso contra Saturnia vultu:
"ista quidem quia nota mihi tua, magne, voluntas,
Iuppiter, et Turnum et terras invita reliqui;
nec tu me aeria solam nunc sede videres   810
digna indigna pati, sed flammis cincta sub ipsa
starem acie traheremque inimica in proelia Teucros.
Iuturnam misero (fateor) succurrere fratri
suasi et pro vita maiora audere probavi,
non ut tela tamen, non ut contenderet arcum;   815
adiuro Stygii caput implacabile fontis,
una superstitio superis quae reddita divis.
et nunc cedo equidem pugnasque exosa relinquo.
illud te, nulla fati quod lege tenetur,
pro Latio obtestor, pro maiestate tuorum: 820
cum iam conubiis pacem felicibus (esto)
component, cum iam leges et foedera iungent,
ne vetus indigenas nomen mutare Latinos
neu Troas fieri iubeas Teucrosque vocari
aut vocem mutare viros aut vertere vestem.   825
sit Latium, sint Albani per saecula reges,
sit Romana potens Itala virtute propago:
occidit, occideritque sinas cum nomine Troia."
olli subridens hominum rerumque repertor:
"es germana Iovis Saturnique altera proles,   830
irarum tantos volvis sub pectore fluctus.
verum age et inceptum frustra submitte furorem
do quod vis, et me victusque volensque remitto.

sermonem Ausonii patrium moresque tenebunt,
utque est nomen erit; commixti corpore tantum 835
subsident Teucri. morem ritusque sacrorum
adiciam faciamque omnes uno ore Latinos.
hinc genus Ausonio mixtum quod sanguine surget,
supra homines, supra ire deos pietate videbis,
nec gens ulla tuos aeque celebrabit honores." 840
adnuit his Iuno et mentem laetata retorsit;
interea excedit caelo nubemque relinquit.

NO ILLUSTRATION FOR LINES 887–918

Aeneas instat contra telumque coruscat
ingens arboreum et saevo sic pectore fatur:
"quae nunc deinde mora est? aut quid iam, Turne, retractas?
non cursu, saevis certandum est comminus armis. 890
verte omnes tete in facies et contrahe quidquid
sive animis sive arte vales; opta ardua pennis
astra sequi clausumve cava te condere terra."
ille caput quassans: "non me tua fervida terrent
dicta, ferox; di me terrent et Iuppiter hostis." 895
nec plura effatus saxum circumspicit ingens,
saxum antiquum ingens, campo quod forte iacebat,
limes agro positus litem ut discerneret arvis.
vix illum lecti bis sex cervice subirent,
qualia nunc hominum producit corpora tellus; 900
ille manu raptum trepida torquebat in hostem
altior insurgens et cursu concitus heros.
sed neque currentem se nec cognoscit euntem
tollentemve manu saxumve immane moventem;
genua labant, gelidus concrevit frigore sanguis. 905
tum lapis ipse viri vacuum per inane volutus
nec spatium evasit totum neque pertulit ictum.
ac velut in somnis, oculos ubi languida pressit
nocte quies, nequiquam avidos extendere cursus
velle videmur et in mediis conatibus aegri 910
succidimus; non lingua valet, non corpore notae
sufficiunt vires nec vox aut verba sequuntur:
sic Turno, quacumque viam virtute petivit,
successum dea dira negat. tum pectore sensus
vertuntur varii; Rutulos aspectat et urbem 915
cunctaturque metu letumque instare tremescit,
nec quo se eripiat, nec qua vi tendat in hostem,
nec currus usquam videt aurigamve sororem.

The Death of Turnus

ILLUSTRATIONS 12.5 A, B, C — THE DEATH OF TURNUS (919–952)

1. What divinities are represented at the top of the illustration? Explain the owl.

2. What two cities are represented in the scene?

3. How do the details of lines 940–947 receive special emphasis in the illustration?

4. How is the earlier wounding of Turnus rendered with particular accuracy?

Write the answers to the questions in the space below.

ILLUSTRATION 12.5, THE DEATH OF TURNUS

Cunctanti telum Aeneas fatale coruscat,
sortitus fortunam oculis, et corpore toto 920
eminus intorquet. murali concita numquam
tormento sic saxa fremunt nec fulmine tanti
dissultant crepitus. volat atri turbinis instar
exitium dirum hasta ferens orasque recludit
loricae et clipei extremos septemplicis orbis; 925
per medium stridens transit femur. incidit ictus
ingens ad terram duplicato poplite Turnus.
consurgunt gemitu Rutuli, totusque remugit
mons circum et vocem late nemora alta remittunt
ille humilis supplexque oculos dextramque precantem 930
protendens "equidem merui nec deprecor" inquit:
"utere sorte tua. miseri te si qua parentis
tangere cura potest, oro (fuit et tibi talis
Anchises genitor) Dauni miserere senectae
et me, seu corpus spoliatum lumine mavis, 935
redde meis. vicisti et victum tendere palmas
Ausonii videre; tua est Lavinia coniunx;
ulterius ne tende odiis." stetit acer in armis
Aeneas, volvens oculos dextramque repressit;
et iam iamque magis cunctantem flectere sermo 940
coeperat, infelix umero cum apparuit alto
balteus et notis fulserunt cingula bullis
Pallantis pueri, victum quem vulnere Turnus
straverat atque umeris inimicum insigne gerebat.
ille, oculis postquam saevi monimenta doloris 945
exuviasque hausit, furiis accensus et ira
terribilis: "tune hinc spoliis indute meorum
eripiare mihi? Pallas te hoc vulnere, Pallas
immolat et poenam scelerato ex sanguine sumit."
hoc dicens ferrum adverso sub pectore condit 950
fervidus; ast illi solvuntur frigore membra
vitaque cum gemitu fugit indignata sub umbras.

APPENDIX

ANNOTATED LIST OF ILLUSTRATIONS FROM DRYDEN

1. Page: 251
   Scene: **The Storm**
   Line: AE. 1. l. 1 (lower left hand corner)
   Attribution: none
   Dedication: To His Royal Highness Prince George of Denmark

2. Page: 260
   Scene: **Landing at Harbor of Carthage**
   Line: AE. 1. l. 295 (lower left hand corner)
   Attribution: none
   Dedication: To Her Royal Highness Princess Anne of Denmark

3. Page: 261
   Scene: **Venus, Jupiter, and Mercury with Carthage Below**
   Line: AE. 1. l. 315 (lower right hand corner)
   Attribution: F. Cleyn in Lombart sculpsit londini (center)
   Dedication: To her Grace Mary Dutchess of Ormond
   Note: plate is between pages 260 and 261 attached to back of illustration of the landing; its blank back faces page 261

4. Page: 264
   Scene: **Aeneas and Achates Meet the Disguised Venus**
   Line: AE. 1. l. 435 (lower right hand corner)
   Attribution: Cleyn in. Lombart sculpsit (lower left hand corner)
   Dedication: To ye Right Hon:^{ble} Anne Countess of Exeter Wife
   to ye Right Hon:^{ble} John Earle of Exeter
   Baron Caecill of Burleigh

5. Page: 276
   Scene: **Aeneas Meets Dido in the Temple of Juno**
   Line: AE. 1. l. 875 (center)
   Attribution: none
   Dedication: To the Right Hon:^{ble} Elizabeth Countess
   Dowager of Winchelsea & ct.

6. Page: 282*
   Scene: **The Banquet in Dido's Palace**
   Line: AE 1. l. 995 (lower left hand corner)
   Attribution: F Cleyn in Lombart sculpsit londini (lower left hand corner into middle)
   Dedication: To the most Honble Ursala
   Marchioness of Normanby
   Note: * In the 1698 Edition page 281 is numbered page 282, while the real page 282 is correctly numbered. This illustration should face page 281.

7.   Page: 284
      Scene: **TheTrojan Horse**
      Line: AE. 2. l. 1 (above attribution)
      Attribution: P Lombart scul A londre (lower right hand corner)
      Dedication: To ye most Illustrious Prince Charles
                     Duke of Somerset Knight of ye most
                     Noble Order of ye Garter
      Note: In Ogilby's 1654 *Aeneid*, an illustration of the Trojan Horse accompanies the opening of Book II. This illustration does not appear in the University of Pennsylvania's 1697 Dryden. In my 1698 Dryden there is evidence that an illustration was attached to face page 282; traces of that page remain in the gutter between 284 and 285 in my copy of 1698 edition. The illustration does appear in the California Dryden. The CD image is taken from the University of Pennsylvania's Ogilby.

8.   Page: 292
      Scene: **Laocoon**
      Line: AE. 2. l. 290 (left of center, bottom)
      Attribution: none
      Dedication: To the Right Hon:^{ble} James
                     Earle of Salisbury &
      Note: My copy of 1698 Dryden is missing the illustration of Laocoon which appeared between pages 292 and 293 and which faced the text of page 292. There is evidence that the illustration has been carelessly removed. The CD image is taken from the University of Pennsylvania's 1697 Dryden.

9.   Page: 300
      Scene: **Troy Invaded**
      Line: AE 2. l. 545 (lower left hand corner)
      Attribution: none
      Dedication: To the Right Hon:^{ble} William O.Bryen Earle
                     of Inchiquin in the Kingdom of Ireland

10.   Page: 307
      Scene: **The Death of Priam**
      Line: AE. 2. l. 755 (center)
      Attribution: Lombart scul. A londre (lower right hand corner)
      Dedication: To ye Right Hon:^{ble} Roger Earle
                     of Orrery Baron of Broghill & ct.

11.   Page: 310
      Scene: **Anchises and the Omen (Flames Appear over the Head of Ascanius)**
      Line: AE 2. l. 925 (lower right hand corner)
      Attribution: F. Cleyn in W. Hollar fecit (lower left hand corner)
      Dedication: To ye Right Hon,^{ble} Rob:^{t} Ld Constable Vis.^{nt}
                     Dunbar in ye Kingdom of Scotland

12. Page: 313
    Scene: **The Escape of Aeneas, Anchises, Ascanius, and Creusa**
    Line: AE. 2. l. 985 (center)
    Attribution: Lombart scul A Londre (lower right hand corner)
    Dedication: To ye Right Hon:^ble Mary Countess
    Earle of Derby & ct L:^d of Man & ye Isles
    Dowager of Northampton

13. Page: 317
    Scene: **Aeneas Pulls Myrtle Branch from Thicket at Enos; Blood of Polydorus**
    Line: AE. 3. l. 1 (lower right hand corner)
    Attribution: F. Cleyn inu W. Hollar fecit.
    Dedication: To the Right Honble William Stanley

14. Page: 320
    Scene: **Apollo on Delos Tells Aeneas to Seek his Ancient Mother**
    Line: AE. 3. l. 110 (lower left hand corner)
    Attribution: Lombart scul A londre (lower right hand corner)
    Dedication: To the Right Hon:^ble Nathanael Lord
    Bishop of Durham

15. Page: 326
    Scene: **Aeneas Confronts Harpies and Celaeno**
    Line: AE. 3. l. 315 (lower right hand corner)
    Attribution: none
    Dedication: To ye Right Reverend Dr. John Hartstonge B;p
    of Ossory in Kilkenny Son of Sr Standish Hartstronge Bar,^t

16. Page: 329
    Scene: **Aeneas Meets Andromache**
    Line: AE. 3. l. 415 (lower right hand corner)
    Attribution: F. Cleyn inu W. Hollar fecit.
    Dedication: To the Hon:^ble D:^r Jo:^n Montague Master of
    Trinity College in Cambridge

17. Page: 336
    Scene: **Aeneas and Ascanius Depart from Andromache**
    Line: AE. 3. l. 625 (lower right hand corner)
    Attribution: F. Cleyn inu W. Hollar fecit. (right of center)
    Dedication: To Edward Browne D.^r in Physick

18. Page: 343
    Scene: **Aeneas Meets the Cyclops**
    Line: AE. 3. l. 865 (lower left hand corner)
    Attribution: none
    Dedication: To Wm Gibbons D.^r in Physick

19. Page: 346
    Scene: **Anna and Dido**
    Line: AE 4. l. 1 (lower left hand corner)
    Attribution: F. Cleyn in P. Lombart sculpsit londini (center bottom of page)
    Dedication: To ye Right Honble John Earle of
                  Exeter Baron Caehcill of Burleigh & ct

20. Page: 348
    Scene: **The Sacrifices of Dido**
    Line: AE. 4. l. 80
    Attribution: F. Cleyn inu Lombart sculpscit londini (center of bottom of page)
    Dedication: To the Lady Giffard

21. Page: 353
    Scene: **Lady Rumor, the Storm in the Hunt, Aeneas and Dido at the Cave**
    Line: AE. 4. l. 230 (lower right hand corner)
    Attribution: Lombart f.pculpit londini [sic]
    Dedication: To The Right Honble Hugh Ld Clifford
                  Baron of Chudleigh in ye County of Devon

22. Page: 357
    Scene: **Mercury Visits Aeneas as he Builds Carthage**
    Line: AE. 4. l. 380 (right of center)
    Attribution: F. Cleyn inu; W. Hollar fecit (lower left hand corner)
    Dedication: To John Walkedon of ye Inner Temple Esq:

23. Page: 368
    Scene: **Preparation of Dido's Funeral Pyre and Offerings to Underworld**
    Line: AE. 4. l. 730 (lower right hand corner)
    Attribution: F. Cleyn in; Lombart sculpsit londini (lower left hand corner)
    Dedication: To Henry Tasburgh Esq of Bodney in ye
                  County of Norfolk

24. Page: 375
    Scene: **The Visitation of Iris**
    Line: AE. 4. l. 990 (center bottom)
    Attribution: none
    Dedication: To ye Lady Bronnlone Daughter & Coheiress of S:^r Richard Mason / K^t. Clerk
                  Comtroler of ye Greencloth to K. Charles ye 2.^d & K.Iames ye 2^d. / Wife to S^r
                  Will: Bronnlone 2.^d Son to S:^r Richard Bronnlone / Bar.^t of Humby in ye County
                  of Lincolnery

25. Page: 377
    Scene: **King Acestes Meets Aeneas and Ascanius upon their Landing in Sicily**
    Line: AE. 5. l. 1 (lower left hand corner)
    Attribution: F.Cleyn inv. W.Hollar fecit (lower right hand corner)
    Dedication: To the most illustrious Prince Charles Duke of
                  St Albans Master Falconer to his Ma.^{ty} and
                  Captaine of ye Honble Band of Gen.^r Pensioners

26. Page: 383
    Scene: **The Boat Race in the Funeral Games**
    Line: AE. 5. l. 150 (right of center bottom)
    Attribution: none
    Dedication: To the Right Hon:^ble Arthur Herbert
                   Earle of Torrington & Baron of Torbay
    Note: This illustration is mounted incorrectly and should be facing page 382 where line
                   150 begins.

27. Page: 390
    Scene: **The Foot Race with Nisus and Euryalus**
    Line: Ae. 5. l. 425 (lower right hand corner)
    Attribution: lombart sculpsit londini (position?)
    Dedication: To Anthony Hammond of Somersham
                   In the County of Huntingdon Esqr.

28. Page: 395
    Scene: **The Gauntlet Fight between Dares and Entellus**
    Line: Ae. 5. l. 590 (lower left hand corner)
    Attribution: F. Cleyn inue, Lombart sculpseit londini (lower right hand corner)
    Dedication: To Henry St John of Lydiard Tregozo Esqr.

29. Page: 396
    Scene: **The Archery Contest**
    Line: AE. 5.l.645 (center bottom)
    Attribution: none
    Dedication: To Stephen Waller D:^r of Laws

30. Page: 399*
    Scene: **The Parade of Riders before the Horse Race**
    Line: AE. 5. l. 720 (center bottom)
    Attribution: none
    Dedication: To ye most illustrious Prince William
                   Duke of Glocester & ct.
    Note: Page is misnumbered as "499."

31. Page: 409
    Scene: **Neptune and Venus Speak to One Another**
    Line: AE. 5. l. 1075 (right of center bottom)
    Attribution: F. Cleyn inv; W. Hollar fecit (lower left hand corner)
    Dedication: To Edmond Waller of Beaconsfield in the
                   County of Bucks Esqb

32. Page: 412
    Scene: **Aeneas and the Sibyl**
    Line: AE. 6. l. 1 (right of center bottom)
    Attribution: f Clein invantor [sic]; P Lombart sculpsit londini (lower left hand corner)
    Dedication: To ye Right Honble Basil Earle of Denbigh Vis-
                   Count Fielding Baron Nenenham Padox & St Lis

33.   Page: 420
       Scene: **Aeneas, Two Doves, and the Golden Bough**
       Line: AE. 6. l. 280 (right of center bottom)
       Attribution: F. Cleyn inv (center), W. Hollar fecit (right of center)
       Dedication: To Sr. Tho. Dyke of Horeham in ye
                    County of Sussex Bart

34.   Page: 421
       Scene: **The Funeral of Misenus**
       Line: AE. 6. l. 310 (bottom right)
       Attribution: f Clien Invenit Lombart sculpsit (left of center)
       Dedication: To Mrs. Anne Baynard Daughter of Dr. Ednd
                    Baynard of the family of Leckham
                    In ye County of Wilts

35.   Page: 424
       Scene: **Underworld Scene: Aeneas, Sibyl, Centaurs, Geryon, Briareus, Hydra,
                    Chimaera**
       Line: AE. 6. l. 390 (left of center)
       Attribution: F. Cleyn inv. (left), W. Hollar fecit (right)
       Dedication: To John Lenknor Esqr. Of West Deane in the
                    County of Sussex

36.   Page: 428
       Scene: **Charon, Aeneas, and Sibyl with Golden Bough**
       Line: AE. 6. l. 550 (near lower left corner)
       Attribution: F. Cleyn inv W Hollar fecit (lower right corner)
       Dedication: To Sr. Fleetwood Sheppard Knight
                    Gent: Usher of ye Black Rod

37.   Page: 430
       Scene: **Aeneas Meets Dido in the Underworld**
       Line: AE. 6. l. 625 (bottom right corner)
       Attribution: Fra Cleyn inu, W Hollar fecit (right of center)
       Dedication: To Gilbert Dolbin of Thindon
                    In Northampton Shire Esq

38.   Page: 432
       Scene: **Deiphobus**
       Line: AE. 6. l. 675 (near lower right corner)
       Attribution: none
       Dedication: To Christopher Knight Esq of Chanton in
                    Hant-shire

39.   Page: 444
       Scene: **Anchises Explains the Parade of Heroes to Aeneas**
       Line: AE. 6. l. 1085 (near bottom left corner)
       Attribution: F. Cleyn in (left of center)
       Dedication: To Robert Harley of Bramton Castle
                    In ye County of Hereford Esq

40. Page: 450
    Scene: **Juno Opening the Temple of Janus**
    Line: AE. 7. l. 1 (left of center)
    Attribution: F. Cleyn in (lower left corner), P Lombart sculpsit londini (right of center)
    Dedication: To the Right Honble Henry Earle of Romney Viscount
                 Sydney of Shippy Baron Milton Master Generall
                 Of the Ordinance Ld Warden of the Cinque Ports &ct

41. Page: 454
    Scene: **The Banquet, "Eating of Tables"**
    Line: AE. 7. l. 250 (right of center)
    Attribution: F Cleyn inv. W. Hollar fecit (lower left corner)
    Dedication: To Anthony Henly of ye Grange in Hantshire Esq:^r

42. Page: 458
    Scene: **The Audience of Latinus**
    Line: AE. 7. l. 290 (bottom right)
    Attribution: none
    Dedication: To George Stepney Esqr His Maties Envoy Extr^{ary}
                 To Severall Princes in Germany and one of
                 The Councill of Trade

43. Page: 466
    Scene: **Juno, Allecto, Amata and Latin Women**
    Line: AE. 7. l. 550 (bottom center)
    Attribution: Fran: Cleyn inv. W. Hollar fec: londini, 1652 (bottom right)
    Dedication: To Coll.^l Thomas Farrington of the
                 Parish of St. James's Westminster

44. Page: 470
    Scene: **Silvia's Stag**
    Line: AE. 7. l. 675 (right edge, just above bottom)
    Attribution: Fran: Cleyn inv. W. Hollar fecit 16?? londini (position?)
    Dedication: To ye Right Honble ye Lady Mary Sackville daughter
                 To Charles Earle of Dorset & Middlesex

45. Page: 478
    Scene: **Catalogue of Italian Forces**
    Line: AE. 7. l. 1075 (left of center)
    Attribution: F. Cleyn inv. W. Hollar fe (center to right of center)
    Dedication: To Charles Fox of ye Parish of
                 St. Martin in ye Fields Esqr

46. Page: 484
    Scene: **Aeneas Dreams of God of Tibur**
    Line: AE. 8. l. 1 (lower right corner, above "londini")
    Attribution: F Cleyn in (left of center), P Lombart sculpsit (right of center), londini (lower right
                 corner)
    Dedication: To ye Right Honble Tho Earle of Ailsbury &
                 Elgin Viscount Bruce of Ampthill Baron Bruce
                 Of Whorleton Shelton and Kinloss &ct.

47.   Page: 497
      Scene: **Evander and Pallas**
      Line: Ene. Ye 8.th l. 450 (left of center)
      Attribution: F Cleyn inv: W. Hollar fecit. (lower right)
      Dedication: To the Honble Robert Bruce Second son to
                     Robert late Earle of Ailesbury

48.   Page: 500
      Scene: **The Forge of the Cyclopes**
      Line: AE. 8. l. 560 (left of center)
      Attribution: F. Cleyn inv: W. Hollar fe (left of center)
      Dedication: To Christopher Rich of Grays Inn Esq.
      Note: In my copy of 1698 Dryden this illustration is appears in the *Georgics*, facing
                     page 198. Because this leaf is damaged, the image on the CD is taken from The
                     University of Pennsylvania's 1697 Dryden.

49.   Page: 508
      Scene: **The Delivery of Shield of Aeneas**
      Line: AE. 8. l. 825 (center)
      Attribution: F. Cleyn inv (lower left), W. Hollar fecit 1653 (lower right)
      Dedication: To Sr. Godfrey Kneller Knight
                     Principall Painter to his Majesty

50.   Page: 514
      Scene: **Iris Visits Turnus**
      Line: AE. 9. l. 1 (center, over Cleyn)
      Attribution: F. Cleyn inv, W. Hollar fecit (center)
      Dedication: To the Right Honble Robert Earle of
                     Sunderland Ld Chamberlaine of his
                     Majesties Household &ct.

51.   Page: 521
      Scene: **Cybele and the Burning of the Ships**
      Line: AE. 9. l. 130 (right)
      Attribution: F. Cleyn in (left), P Lombart londini (center)
      Dedication: To Thomas Foley Junr Of Great Witley Court in
                     In the County of Worcester Esq.
      Note: plate is placed at line 230

52.   Page: 527
      Scene: **The Raid of Nisus and Euryalus**
      Line: AE. 9. l. 435 (lower right corner)
      Attribution: none
      Dedication: To ye Honble Colonel George Cholmondeley
                     Colonel of his Majestys Troop of Granadier
                     Guards and Groom of his Maj^ties Bedchamber

53. Page: 531
    Scene: **Nisus Stabs Volscens in Mouth**
    Line: AE. l. 590 (bottom right corner)
    Attribution: F. Cleyn detin, W. Hollar fecit (just left of center)
    Dedication: To Sr. Jon Percivale Bart. of Burton
    in the County of Corke in Ireland

54. Page: 536
    Scene: **Turnus Pursues Lycus at the Tower Wall**
    Line: AE. 9. l. 750 (bottom right corner)
    Attribution: F. Cleyn in P Lombart londini (center)
    Dedication: To Coll.¹ Christopher Codrington one of the Captains in his Maties
    First Regiment of foot Guards

55. Page: 544
    Scene: **Turnus Splits Open the Head of Pandarus**
    Line: AE. 9. l. 1010 (bottom right corner)
    Attribution: F. Cleyn inu: W. Hollar fecit (left of center)
    Dedication: To Mr. John Closterman

56. Page: 548
    Scene: *Concilium Deorum*
    Line: AE. 10. l. 1 (center, below attribution)
    Attribution: F. Cleyn in P Lombart sculpsit londini (center)
    Dedication: To ye Right Honble Iohn Ld Viscount Fitzharding of
    Beare-haven and Baron Berkley of Rathdowne
    In ye Kingdom of Ireland & Master of ye Horse to
    Her Royall Highness the Princess Anne of Denmark

57. Page: 561
    Scene: **Venus Protects Aeneas in Battle**
    Line: AE. 10. l. 450 (right of center)
    Attribution: F. Cleyn inv: W. Hollar fecit (right)
    Dedication: To ye Right Honble Sr. Robert Howard
    Auditor of his Maties Exchequer, and one of ye
    Lords of his Maj^ties most Honble Privy Councill

58. Page: 568
    Scene: **Turnus Takes the Belt of Pallas**
    Line: AE. 10. l. 690 (left of center)
    Attribution: F. Cleyn in P Lombart sculpsit londini (right of center)
    Dedication: To Sr. Iohn Leveson Gower of Trentham in
    Staffordshire Baronet

59. Page: 578
    Scene: **Lausus Protects Mezentius from Aeneas**
    Line: AE. 10. l. 1125 (left of center)
    Attribution: F. Cleyn inv: W. Hollar fecit (right)
    Dedication: To Sr. Charles Orby Baronet of Burton
    Pedwarden in ye County of Lincolne
    Note: Plate is placed at line 1025

60.   Page: 583
        Scene: **Aeneas Attacks Mezentius**
        Line: AE. 10. l. 1275 (left of center)
        Attribution: F. Cleyn in P Lombart [space] sculpsit londini (center)
        Dedication: To Tho. Hopkins of ye Middle Temple Esqr
        Note: Plate is placed at line 1175

61.   Page: 588
        Scene: **Aeneas Displays Spoils of Mezentius, Addresses Troops**
        Line: AE. 11. l. 1 (right of center)
        Attribution: F. Cleyn inv: W. Hollar fecit (slightly left of center)
        Dedication: To ye Right Noble Charles Duke of Shrewsbury Marquis of Alton Earle / Of
                        Shrewsbury Wexford & Water-ford, Baron Talbot Strange of / Blackmere Gifford
                        of Brimsfield &ct One of the Lords of his Maties / Most honble Privy Councill
                        Principall Secretary of State and Knight / Of ye most Noble Order of the Garter.

62.   Page: 594
        Scene: **The Funeral Procession of Pallas**
        Line: AE. 11. l. 215 (bottom right corner)
        Attribution: F. Cleyn in P Lombart sculpsit londini (left of center)
        Dedication: To Sr. Walter Kirkham Blount of Sodington
                        In the County of Worcester Bart.

63.   Page: 596
        Scene: **The Funeral Pyre of Pallas**
        Line: AE. 11. l. 290 (center)
        Attribution: F. Cleyn inv: [space] W. Hollar fecit (right of center)
        Dedication: To ye Honble John Noel Esq 2^d Son to Rt. Honble
                        Baptist late Ld Viscount Campden Baron of
                        Ridlington & Ilmington

64.   Page: 599
        Scene: **The Council of Latinus**
        Line: AE. 11. l. 365 (center)
        Attribution: none
        Dedication: To ye Most Honble John Marquis of Normanby
                        Earle of Mulgrave & Kt. of ye most noble Order of ye Garter
        Note: Corresponds to Latin lines 11.343–350

65.   Page: 618
        Scene: **Camilla Kills Aunus**
        Line: AE. 11. l. 1035 (lower right corner)
        Attribution: F. Cleyn inv (left corner), W. Hollar fecit, 1653 (right of center)
        Dedication: To the Right Hon.ble William Berkley
                        Baron Barkley of Stratton &ct.
        Note: The plate is inserted backwards

66. Page: 619
    Scene: **The Death of Camilla**
    Line: AE. l. 1150 (right of center)
    Attribution: none
    Dedication: To Arthur Manwaringe of Ightfield in the
                 County of Salop Esq.[r]

67. Page: 628
    Scene: **Turnus in the Court of Latinus**
    Line: AE. 12. l. 1. (left of center)
    Attribution: F.Cleyn inu. W. Hollar fecit. (bottom right corner)
    Dedication: To the Right Hon:[ble] Phillip Lord Stanhope
                 Earle of Chesterfield Baron of Shelford in
                 The Kingdom of England

68. Page: 635
    Scene: **Latinus at the Altar with Aeneas, Ascanius, Turnus**
    Line: AE. 12. l. 250 (bottom right)
    Attribution: F. Cleyn in Lombart sculpscit londini (bottom center)
    Dedication: To ye Hon.[ble] Brigadier Edward Fitzpatrick

69. Page: 645
    Scene: **Venus Heals Aeneas's Wound**
    Line: En 12. l. 570 (bottom right hand corner of decidation)
    Attribution: F.Cleyn inv W. Carter fecit (bottom left)
    Dedication: To Thomas Hobbs
                 D:[r] in Physic

    70. Page: 661
    Scene: **The Gods on Olympus, Aeneas Extracts a Spear**
    Line: Aen 12. l. 1120 (bottom right of dedication)
    Attribution: F.Cleyn inv W. Hollar fecit (bottom right of center)
    Dedication: To the Right Hon:[ble] Francis North
                 Baron of Guilford

71. Page: 668
    Scene: **The Death of Turnus**
    Line: AEn 12. l. 1360 (bottom right of dedication)
    Attribution: Cleyn inv W.Faithorne fe (bottom right of center)
    Dedication: To his Grace James Duke of Ormond
                 Chancellor of the Universitys of Oxford
                 And Dublin Knight of the most Noble Order
                 of the Garter Soc:

STUDENT NOTES

STUDENT NOTES

Vergil Texts & Ancillae

**Vergil's Aeneid
Selections from Books 1, 2, 4, 6, 10, and 12**
Barbara Weiden Boyd
2nd Edition Student Text: (2004)
Paperback, ISBN 0-86516-584-X
Hardbound, ISBN 0-86516-583-1

1st Edition Teacher's Guide: (2002)
Paperback, ISBN 0-86516-481-9

**Why Vergil?
A Collection of
Interpretations**
Stephanie Quinn, ed.
(2000)
Paperback, ISBN 0-86516-418-5
Hardbound, ISBN 0-86516-435-5

**Vergil's Aeneid:
Books I–VI**
Clyde Pharr
Illus., xvii + 518 pp. + fold-out
(1964, Reprint 1998)
Paperback, ISBN 086516-421-5
Hardbound, ISBN 086516-433-9

**Vergil's Dido & Mimus
Magicus**
Composed by Jan Novák;
Conducted by Rafael Kubelik
Performed by the Symphony
Orchestra of the Bayerischer
Rundfunk (Germany)
Original record published by
audite Schallplatten, Germany
Limited Edition CD (1997) 40-page libretto in Latin,
English, and German, ISBN 0-86516-346-4

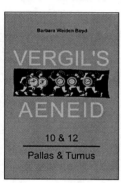

**Vergil's Aeneid, 10 & 12
Pallas & Turnus**
Barbara Weiden Boyd
Student Text: xii + 44 pp. (1998)
Paperback, ISBN 0-86516-415-0
Teacher's Guide: vi + 13 pp. (1998)
Paperback, ISBN 0-86516-428-2

**The Labors of Aeneas
What A Pain It Was to
Found the Roman Race**
Rose Williams
Pages: vi + 108, (2003), 6" x 9"
Paperback,
ISBN 0-86516-556-4

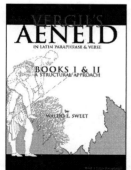

**Vergil's Aeneid:
Books I and II**
Waldo E. Sweet
Transitional Book
163 pp. (1960, Reprint 1983)
Paperback, ISBN 0-86516-023-6

**Servius' Commentary
on Book Four of Vergil's
Aeneid**
An Annotated Translation
**Christopher M. McDonough,
Richard E. Prior, and
Mark Stansbury**
Pages: xviii + 170, (2003), 6" x 9"
Paperback
ISBN 0-86516-514-9

Bolchazy-Carducci Publishers, Inc.
www.BOLCHAZY.com

Instructions: Poet & Artist, Imaging the Aeneid CD

Contents of the CD
- PowerPoint Presentation files
- PowerPoint Viewer for Windows
- PowerPoint Viewer for MAC
- PDF files that can be read with Adobe Acrobat Reader®
- Adobe Acrobat Reader®

For Windows® (PC) Computer Users

After putting the CD into the drive, open the folder titled "Poet & Artist Presentation." Double click on one of the Microsoft PowerPoint files. If you have Microsoft PowerPoint software installed on your computer, the file will open with the Microsoft PowerPoint application. If you do not have Microsoft PowerPoint software installed on your computer, the Microsoft PowerPoint viewer will automatically open the presentation.

For Macintosh® Computer Users

After putting the CD into the drive, open the folder titled "Poet & Artist Presentation." Double click on one of the Microsoft PowerPoint files. If you have Microsoft PowerPoint software installed on your computer, the file will open with the Microsoft PowerPoint application. If you do not have the Microsoft PowerPoint software installed on your computer, you will need to double click on the "Microsoft PowerPoint Viewer" icon to open the viewer software. Then under the "file" menu, select "Open" and select the PowerPoint file you would like to view.

For PDF File Users

All of the Microsoft PowerPoint Presentation files have been converted to PDF documents. If you are viewing these images in the PDF format, use the "arrow" icons at the bottom of the window to advance to the next slide. If you do not have Adobe Acrobat Reader on your computer, it is available on this CD.